Checklist for Starting a Business

This checklist provides the basic steps you should think about when starting a business and is not to be construed as all-inclusive. Other steps may be appropriate for your specific type of business.

☐ Prepare your business plan

If you're starting a new business or trying to obtain capital for expansion, this is your first and most important step. *See page 8*

☐ Seek legal advice

Consult an attorney about your business form of ownership. Leases, contracts laws and regulations affect every aspect of business strategy. Online source for legal and regulatory information is **www.Business.gov** *See page 3*

☐ Choose business structure

Consider legal and tax implications. Obtain legal advice before making this decision. *See page 3*.

☐ Financing options

All businesses must raise sufficient capital. Start-up resources can include family and friends, personal savings, owner financing, and business loans. *See page 14-19, 25*

☐ Obtain licenses and permits

State Business License – Washington's one-stop registration process requires filing a Master Business Application to obtain a UBI (Unified Business Identifier) number and to register trade names. File for Washington State at **www.dol.gov**. For Idaho at **www.sos.idaho.gov**. *See page 4*

Specialty Licenses – A list of business activities that require specialty licensing, permits or certifications are listed at www.dol.wa.gov/business. Dept of Licensing Master License Service 360-664-1400. See page 4

Local Licenses and Permits - You may need to get a city license and/or county permit for each place where you do business. Check with your local government regarding zoning and building code regulations. Contact your local department of licensing or city clerk's office for more information.

☐ Determine regulatory and record-keeping requirements

Environmental Regulations – Find out which state and federal environmental permits are needed for your business, visit the WA Department of Ecology's On-line Permit Assistance System (OPAS) at **www.ecy.wa.gov** or call 360-407-6000. Access Idaho Dept of Environmental Quality online at **www.deq.state.id.us**.

Fire Regulations – Contact your local fire officials.

Health Regulations – Contact your local health department regarding sewer, water and solid waste utilities.

Industrial Health & Safety Regulations – Contact the Dept of Labor & Industries/Division of Industrial Safety and Health at 1-800-423-7233 or visit their web site at **www.lni.wa.gov/wisha.** In Idaho go to **www.boisestate.edu/OSHCon/** or call 208-426-3283.

Industrial Insurance – For information on hiring, insurance, and tax withholding for employees, contact the Dept of Labor & Industries/Division of Industrial Insurance at 1-800-547-8367 or 360-956-4817. **www.lni.wa.gov**
For Idaho contact the Idaho Industrial Commission **www.iic.idaho.gov**

New Hire Reporting – Report each newly hired or rehired employee to WA Department of Social and Health Services (DSHS) at 1-800-562-0479. **www.dshs.wa.gov/newhire**

State and Federal Taxes – These vary with the form, nature and location of your business. Refer questions about Washington State taxes to the Dept of Revenue **www.dor.wa.gov** In Idaho access the Idaho State Tax Commission at **www.tax.idaho.gov**. For federal tax info, call 1-800-829-1040 Obtain forms by calling 1-800-829-3676 or downloaded from the IRS web site at **www.irs.gov/smallbiz** *See page 5*

Unemployment Insurance – Refer questions about unemployment insurance for your employees to the WA Employment Security Department at 360-902-9551. **http://www.esd.wa.gov/.** Idaho Works at **http://labor.idaho.gov/iw/**

Wage Regulations & Posters – Required workplace posters are available online at **www.lni.wa.gov/IPUB/101-054-000.asp or** contact the WA State Dept of Labor and Industries/Employment Standards at 1-800-547-8367 or 360-902-4817. In Idaho, go to **http://labor.idaho.gov** or call 208-332-3570.

☐ Business Insurance

Consult with your insurance agent about fire, automobile employee health, bonding, life, and fidelity insurance against employee theft, burglary, vandalism, business interruption, and key person insurance. *See page 9*

☐ Decide on your bookkeeping and accounting system

For information on bookkeeping systems, income tax planning, or income tax returns, consult your accountant, SCORE, SBDC or WBC office, or community college. IRS Publication 583, "Starting a Business and Keeping Records" is helpful. **www.irs.gov/pub/irs-pdf/p583.pdf**

On the Upside...

For the right person, the advantages of business ownership far outweigh the risks.

You get to be your own boss.

Hard work and long hours directly benefit you, rather than increasing profits for someone else.

Earning and growth potential are far less limited.

A new venture is exciting.

Running a business will provide endless variety and challenge and won't settle into a dull routine.

Selecting the Right Legal Structure for Your Company

by Stacey L. Romberg, Attorney at Law - www.staceyromberg.com

Forming a new business can be overwhelming! Hiring employees, leasing commercial space, marketing, selling the product or performing the service is an amazing process. Your decision regarding business formation is an important first step.

What type of entity works best for your business?

There are four **basic types of business entities**: sole proprietorships, partnerships, corporations and limited liability companies (LLC's). Other types of business entities which are beyond the scope of this article, include: limited partnerships, professional service corporations and professional limited liability companies.

A **sole proprietorship** is a common, simple type of business ownership. If you are in business by yourself and obtain your business license, you are a sole proprietor. A sole proprietorship is an appropriate and proper form of business ownership for many small businesses. For federal income tax purposes, the income from the business flows through to the individual, and is reported on the business owner's Schedule C. A sole proprietorship offers no protection from individual liability, so it is essential for sole proprietorships to maintain adequate insurance coverage.

A **partnership** is similar to a sole proprietorship. If you are in business with at least one other person, and obtain your business license, you have a partnership. The partnership exists regardless of whether the partners have formalized their relationship by executing a partnership agreement. A partnership agreement sets forth the rights and obligations of each party, and describe what would happen if a partner dies or wants to sell his or her interest in the business. A partnership, similar to a sole proprietorship, results in federal income tax liability flowing from the entity to the individual partners. A partnership tax return is required, but each individual partner pays his or her share of the business taxes instead of the business itself paying the tax. As in a sole proprietorship, a partnership offers no protection from individual liability.

A **corporation** is formed by filing Articles of Incorporation with the Secretary of State's office. One or more individuals can create a corporation. A key initial decision in forming a corporation is whether it should be a C-Corporation or an S-Corporation. A C-Corporation pays federal taxes both on the corporate level, and on the level of individual shareholders. An S-Corporation pays taxes only on the shareholder level. Certain qualifications must be met in order to register as an S-Corporation. Unlike a sole proprietorship or a partnership, a corporation which is properly formed and maintained can offer protections against individual liability. In order to form and maintain a corporation, you need to retain both an accountant and an attorney to comply with complex tax requirements and corporate formalities set forth in state Revised Codes.

A **limited liability company, or LLC**, is formed by filing a Certificate of Formation with the Secretary of State's office. One or more individuals can create an LLC. An LLC may be taxed in different ways. Consult with your accountant in order to make an informed decision about how your LLC will be taxed, and file the corresponding documents with the IRS. Similar to a corporation, a properly formed and maintained LLC can offer protections against individual liability. Also, you need to retain both an accountant and an attorney in forming an LLC. An attorney can help you prepare key documents, including the LLC Operating Agreement.

Taking a simplistic approach there are **two key factors** *to examine:*

1. What types of potential liabilities does my business face, and can I purchase adequate insurance coverage to handle these liabilities?

2. What tax savings would I receive from forming a business entity?

In analyzing these two factors, you need the help of your "Formation Team," consisting of three key professionals: a business attorney, an accountant and a commercial insurance broker. First, your commercial insurance broker will advise you regarding the potential risks faced by your business, and will help you determine the types of coverage available. Your broker will help you answer the question: Is it helpful and/or necessary to form a business entity, such as a corporation or a limited liability company, in order to decrease the risk of personal liability related to my business?

Second, your accountant can help you answer the question: Is it financially beneficial for me to form a business entity, such as a corporation or a limited liability company, in order to decrease my tax liability? If so, the follow up questions to ask your accountant are: What type of entity would work the best for my particular situation? How will that entity be taxed? What on-going accounting respons bilities do I need to meet?

Third, your business attorney can help you answer the question: How do I form a business entity? Your attorney can explain to you the nature of what you are forming. And, your attorney can explain to you how to operate and maintain the entity, once formed, in a way that minimizes the chances that your personal assets could be at risk for a business-related liability.

To beat the odds and ensure success for your business, you need to be smart about your strengths and weaknesses. You cannot do it all and be successful! Assemble your "Formation Team" of an accountant, an attorney and a commercial insurance broker; and consult with your team continually in the formation of your business. Work with your team to develop a thriving and profitable new venture!

Office of the Secretary of State - www.sos.wa.gov/corps
Corporations Division - 360-753-7115
Register a corporation or limited partnership

Legal Resources

Bar Association -
  King County Lawyer Referral Services - 206-623-2551
  Tacoma/Pierce County - 253-383-3432
  Washington State - www.wsba.org
                   800-945-WSBA or 206-443-WSBA

Entrepreneurial Law Clinic (ELC) - UW School of Law
www.law.washington.edu/Clinics/Entrepreneurial.html
2815 Eastlake Ave E. Suite 300, Seattle, WA 98102
206-336-5616; elcinfo@u.washington.edu
Legal assistance to low-income entrepreneurs in economically distressed communities, and pre-funded high-tech start ups by a team of law students and pro-bono attorneys. Income determines eligibility.

Sirti IP/BizNet - The University District - www.sirti.org
665 North Riverpoint Blvd., Spokane, WA 99202-1665
509-358-2000
Sirti IP/BizNet provides legal services for both start-ups and high-growth technology businesses. Legal services are performed by Gonzaga University law students supervised by expert attorneys at local firms that focus on business and/or intellectual property law.

Idaho State Bar & Idaho Law Foundation, Inc
http://www.isb.idaho.gov/   208-334-4500

Business Licensing Made Easy

There are many types of business licenses, state and local as well as professional. Most businesses are required to have a state license of some sort. Contact your City Clerk's Office and County Business License Office for more information on local licenses and permit requirements.

Check your local Planning Department to ensure your business site meets appropriate zoning requirements. Check your local Building Department to obtain permits for permanent buildings or additions to existing facilities. Check your County Health Department if your business deals with the sale of food.

Washington State Department of Licensing
Master License Service (MLS)
http://www.dol.wa.gov/business/
PO Box 9034 (Physical address: 405 Black Lake Blvd, Bldg 2)
Olympia WA 98507-9034
360-664-1400
The Master Business Application is a simplified application used to apply for many state licenses, registrations and permits, as well as some city licenses. Receive customized licensing information online by accessing **http://www.dol.wa.gov/business/licensing.html**, click on Business Licensing Guide, and submit information relevant to your pending company operation.

Applying for a license will also provide you with a Unified Business Identifier (UBI) number. A UBI number is a nine-digit number that registers you with several state agencies. It is also called a tax registration number, a business registration number, and a business license number.

Filing online is not recommended for some businesses. If your business needs **specialty licenses,** including liquor or lottery licenses, you should file your application by mail. Information about specialty license requirements are posted online at **www.dol.wa.gov/business/specialtylicenses.html.**

City Business License Application
http://access.wa.gov/business/citylicenses.aspx
Most cities and some counties require a business license or permits if the business is located in the city or county limits OR does business there, regardless of the physical location of the business. Some city licenses can be obtained in applying for your state license. For others, contact the local city business license office.

Contractor's Registration
Department of Labor & Industries
www.lni.wa.gov/tradeslicensing/default.asp
1-800-647-0982
This license is required for any person to submit any bid offer to do any work as a construction contractor within Washington State. Applications may be obtained from satellite offices of the Dept of Labor and Industries throughout Washington State. Contractors also need bond and liability insurance coverage.

www.business.idaho.gov
The State of Idaho requires businesses to register with the Idaho Secretary of State and other regulatory agencies. Businesses in Idaho can go to **www.business.idaho.gov** to access all the relevant links for starting, running, relocating, and even closing!

Trade Name Search
A trade name is any name used in the course of business that does not include the full legal name of all the owners of the business. In the case of a limited partnership, corporation or LLC, it is any name that differs in any respect from the name registered with the Secretary of State. Trade names are registered in Washington state by using the Master Business Application. Register as many names as you wish on the paper application. Online you are limited to a total of five names per application.

The purpose of a trade name registration is to provide a record of all owners of a business. The right to use a trade name belongs to the one who first uses it in connection with their business. A trade name will remain registered indefinitely until the owner requests that it be cancelled.

You can find trade name registrations in Washington online with the state's Business and Professional License Search at
https://fortress.wa.gov/dol/dolprod/bpdLicenseQuery
To request a search by mail, send a letter with your return address, a list of names you want to research, and a check of money order to pay the fee of $4 to search up to 3 names. Mail your request to the Master License Service address listed above.

Note: A search result of "No matches were found for your search" does not guarantee that the name is not being used, only that is has not been registered.

Business Name and Record searches:

Washington State Department of Revenue
http://dor.wa.gov/content/doingbusiness/registermybusiness/brd/
Includes some trade names and is intended for use by the public as a consumer protection program.

Washington's Secretary of State
http://www.sos.wa.gov/corps/search.aspx
Find corporation and limited liability company names.

U.S. Patent and Trademark Commission
http://www.uspto.gov/main/profiles/acadres.htm
Contains federally registered names.

http://www.uspto.gov/main/profiles/acadres.htm
FAQ's about trade names

> *Customized business wizards provide license and form information.*
>
> **Washington State**
> **www.dol.wa.gov/business/licensing.html**
>   click on "Business Licensing Guide"
>
> **Idaho**
> **www.idahobizhelp.org**

Regulations and Your Business

It may be inconceivable that your home-based business or part-time enterprise must comply with the numerous local, state and federal regulations, but in all likelihood it will. Don't ignore regulatory details. Doing so may avert some red tape in the short term, but could be an obstacle as your business grows.

Most businesses must obtain one or more licenses and permits from local, state and federal agencies. The licenses or permits required for your business will be determined by your type of business, its organizational structure, and location.

Federal Agencies

Internal Revenue Service (IRS)
www.irs.gov
Tax questions? 1-800-829-4933
To order forms 1-800-829-3676
www.irs.gov/businesses/small/index.html
The Small Business and Self-Employed Tax Center answers questions new business owners have about federal taxes.

Visit the IRS Online Learning and Educational link to see a list of small business video and audio presentations, and other learning tools.

Other relevant IRS topics to explore:
Business Structures: When starting a business, you must decide what form of business entity to establish – this determines which income tax return form you file.

Self-Employment Tax: Everyone must pay Social Security and Medicare Taxes. If you are self-employed, your Social Security/Medicare contribution is made through the self-employment Tax. Payments are made quarterly as part of your estimated tax payments (Form 1040-ES).

Businesses with Employees: Withhold income tax, Social Security and Medicare (FICA), as well as pay the employer's portion of Social Security taxes and pay federal unemployment tax under certain circumstances. Nonpayment of federal taxes can result in audits, penalties, difficulties obtaining bank financing, and closure of your business. See page 7.

Employer Identification Number (EIN): Employers and most types of businesses are required to have an Employer Identification Number (EIN). Apply for an EIN online, search EIN at **www.irs.gov**

IRS Business & Specialty Tax Line
1-800-829-4933, M–F, 7 a.m.–10 p.m. PST.

OSHA Occupational Safety & Health Administration - www.osha.gov
A division of the U.S. Dept. of Labor that regulates working conditions.

Employer Wage Reporting Service Center
www.ssa.gov/employer   1-800-772-6270
Help with all your wage filing responsbilities.

Social Security Administration
www.ssa.gov   1-800-772-1213
Nearly all employees, employers and self-employed persons are required to participate in the social security program. Employers are required to withhold a fixed percentage of employee wages, match each employee's contribution and make periodic deposits to the IRS. Self-employed persons must also make contributions.

U.S. Citizenship and Immigration Services (USCIS) - www.uscis.gov
1-800-357-2099
Employers must fill out an Immigration Form I-9 for each employee hired for both citizens and non-citizens. Form I-9 must be kept by the employer either three years after the date of hire or for one year after employment is terminated, whichever is later. Download current I-9 form from the USCIS website.

U.S. Census Bureau - www.census.gov
The leading source of quality data about the nation's people and economy.

U.S. Department of Labor (DOL)
www.dol.gov   1-866-487-9243
Regulates working conditions, wages, and payment practices.

Washington State Agencies

Department of Revenue
www.dor.wa.gov
Telephone Information Center
1-800-647-7706
Answers most common tax questions.

Copies of publications, laws and rules
www.dor.wa.gov
1-800-647-7706

Business Outreach Workshops
Workshops covering business registration, reporting, tax laws and rules, and recordkeeping requirements are posted online.

The Electronic Filing System (ELF)
www.dor.wa.gov
1-877-FILE ELF (1-877-345-3353)
This free system wa ks filers through a customized return, calculates taxes automatically, flags errors and omissions before a return is filed, and provides instant online access to the latest tax information. ELF's electronic funds transfer lets taxpayers file their tax returns early, but postpone payment until the due date.

Employment Security Dept.
www.esd.wa.gov 360-902-9360
Unemployment Insurance Registration
Required from businesses employing one or more persons. Employers must file quarterly reports showing total wages paid, individual employee earnings, social security numbers, hours worked and tax due with payment.

Labor and Industries
www.lni.wa.gov
Industrial Insurance Registration

www.lni.wa.gov/Main/RunBusiness.asp
360-902-4817
Required for businesses employing one or more persons. Registration authorizes deductions of medical aid and supplemental pension premiums from employee's wages and establishes premium payment accounts for industrial insurance, supplemental pension and medical aid.

Office of the Secretary of State
www.sos.wa.gov/corps
Corporations Division
360-753-7115; TDD: 360-753-1485
Registers business-related entities, corporations, partnerships, limited liability companies, and state trademarks.

Corporate Registration, Profit/Nonprofit Corporations
360-753-7115
WA applicants must file with Secretary of State's Office. This does not relieve applicants from responsibility of also registering with state taxing authorities.

County Regulations

Partnership Recording
(General Partnerships only) Persons starting a general partnership should have a written partnership agreement and buy/sell agreement - reviewed by an attorney.

King 206-296-1570
http://www.kingcounty.gov/business.aspx

Pierce 253-798-7440
www.co.pierce.wa.us/auditor

Snohomish 425-388-3483
www.co.snohomish.wa.us/auditor

Application for Certificate of Registration
Contact County Business License Office to see if your business needs to be registered.

King County 206-296-3504
Pierce County 253-798-7445
Snohomish County 425-388-3627

Idaho Agencies

www.idahobizhelp.org
To obtain a customized list of regulating agencies that you may need to contact for specific business activity, access the **Business Wizard** section of this website.

Bureau of Occupational Licenses
www.ibol.idaho.gov 208-334-3233
Specialty licensing in a variety of occupations. Not all licensing boards contract with the **Bureau of Occupational Licenses**. To find the website of the state agency related to your business visit **www.accessidaho.org/topical.html**

Idaho Dept. Commerce
www.commerce.idaho.gov 208-334-2470
Supports Idaho business formation and expansion.

Idaho Dept of Environmental Quality
www.deq.state.id.us 208-373-0502
Responsible for implementing environmental protection laws and programs. Information about air, water and waste programs, info on permits, regulations and DEQ publications.

Idaho Industrial Commission
www.iic.idaho.gov 208-332-3570
Administers the Idaho Workers' Compensation Law.

Idaho Dept. of Labor
www.labor.idaho.gov 208-332-3570
Assists businesses in solving employment and training related challenges.

Idaho Occupational Safety & Health Consultation Program
www.boisestate.edu/OSHCon
208-426-3283
This free service assists with OSHA safety and health regulations compliance. Safety and industrial hygiene consultants will develop a confidential written report of recommendations. No citations are issued or penalties are assessed. The business owner's obligation is to correct all serious hazards within a reasonable timeframe.

Idaho Secretary of State
www.sos.idaho.gov
208-334-2300
Registration of business entities such as Partnerships, Corporations, and Limited Liability Companies, trademark searches and registration for Idaho State. Also deals with registration of Assumed Business Names – referred to as DBA or Doing Business As.

Idaho State Tax Commission
www.tax.idaho.gov
Administers Idaho state tax laws and provides tax info and education to the public.

County Websites
Go to Idaho Association of Counties **www.idcounties.org** and click on "Counties"

Are You Running a Business or Engaging in a Hobby?

Internal Revenue Service guidelines determine whether an activity is a business or a hobby, an activity not engaged in for profit.

Here are the rules for determining if an activity qualifies as a business and what limitations apply if the activity is not a business.

Taxpayers may deduct ordinary and necessary expenses for conducting a trade or business. An ordinary expense is an expense that is common and accepted in the taxpayer's trade or business. A necessary expense is one that is appropriate for the business. Generally, an activity qualifies as a business if it is carried on with the reasonable expectation of earning a profit.

In order to make this determination, taxpayers should consider the following factors:

- Does the time and effort put into the activity indicate an intention to make a profit?
- Does the taxpayer depend on income from the activity?
- If there are losses, are they due to circumstances beyond the taxpayer's control or did they occur in the start-up phase of the business?
- Has the taxpayer changed methods of operation to improve profitability?
- Does the taxpayer or his/her advisors have the knowledge needed to carry on the activity as a successful business?
- Has the taxpayer made a profit in similar activities in the past?
- Does the activity make a profit in some years?
- Can the taxpayer expect to make a profit in the future from the appreciation of assets used in the activity?

The IRS presumes that an activity is carried on for profit if it makes a profit during at least three of the last five tax years, including the current year — at least two of the last seven years for activities that consist primarily of breeding, showing, training or racing horses.

If an activity is not for profit, losses from that activity may not be used to offset other income. An activity produces a loss when related expenses exceed income. The limit on not-for-profit losses applies to individuals, partnerships, estates, trusts, and S corporations. It does not apply to corporations other than S corporations.

Deductions for hobby activities are claimed as itemized deductions on Schedule A (Form 1040). These deductions must be taken in the following order and only to the extent stated in each of three categories:

- Deductions that a taxpayer may take for personal as well as business activities, such as home mortgage interest and taxes, may be taken in full.
- Deductions that don't result in an adjustment to basis, such as advertising, insurance premiums and wages, may be taken next, to the extent gross income for the activity is more than the deductions from the first category.
- Business deductions that reduce the basis of property, such as depreciation and amortization, are taken last, but only to the extent gross income for the activity is more than the deductions taken in the first two categories.

www.irs.gov

Self-Employment Tax

Self-employment tax (SE tax) is a social security and Medicare tax primarily for individuals who work for themselves.

It is similar to the **Social Security and Medicare taxes** withheld from the pay of most wage earners. The list of items below should not be construed as all-inclusive. Other information may be appropriate for your specific type of business.

You figure SE tax yourself using Schedule SE (Form 1040). Social Security and Medicare taxes of most wage earners are figured by their employers. Also you can deduct half of your SE tax in figuring your adjusted gross income. Wage earners cannot deduct social security and Medicare taxes.

SE tax rate. The self-employment tax rate is 15.3%. The rate consists of two parts: 12.4% for social security (old-age, survivors, and disability insurance) and 2.9% for Medicare (hospital insurance).

Maximum earnings subject to SE tax. Only the first $102,000 of your combined wages, tips, and net earnings in 2008 is subject to any combination of the 12.4% social security part of SE tax, social security tax, or railroad retirement (tier 1) tax.

All your combined wages, tips, and net earnings in 2008 are subject to any combination of the 2.9% Medicare part of SE tax, social security tax, or railroad retirement (tier 1) tax.

Fiscal year filer. If you use a tax year other than the calendar year, you must use the tax rate and maximum earnings limit in effect at the beginning of your tax year. Even if the tax rate or maximum earnings limit changes during your tax year, continue to use the same rate and limit throughout your tax year.

Self-employment tax deduction. You can deduct half of your SE tax in figuring your adjusted gross income. This deduction only affects your income tax. It does not affect either your net earnings from self-employment or your SE tax.

How to Pay Self-Employment Tax

To pay SE tax, you must have a social security number (SSN) or an individual taxpayer identification number (ITIN). Obtaining a Social Security Number. If you never had an SSN, apply for one using Form SS-5, Application for a Social Security Card. You can get this form at any Social Security office or by calling (800) 772-1213. Download the forms at **www.ssa.gov**.

Obtaining an Individual Taxpayer Identification Number. The IRS will issue you an ITIN if you are a nonresident or resident alien and you do not have and are not eligible to get an SSN. To apply for an ITIN , file Form W-7, Application for IRS Individual Taxpayer Identification Number.

Estimated Taxes

Federal income tax is a pay-as-you-go tax. You must pay the tax as you earn or receive income during the year. You generally have to make estimated tax payments if you expect to owe tax, including SE tax, of $1,000 or more when you file your return. There are two ways to pay as you go: withholding and estimated taxes. If you are a self-employed individual and do not have income tax withheld, you must make estimated tax payments.

Who Must Pay Self-Employment Tax?

You must pay SE tax and file Schedule SE (Form 1040) if either of the following applies.

- Your net earnings from self-employment (excluding church employee income) were $400 or more.
- You had church employee income of $108.28 or more.
- Your net earnings from self-employment are based on your earnings subject to SE tax. Most earnings from self-employment are subject to SE tax. Some earnings from employment (certain earnings that are not subject to social security and Medicare taxes) are subject to SE tax.

Note: The SE tax rules apply no matter how old you are and even if you are already receiving social Security or Medicare.

Are You Self-Employed?

You are self-employed if any of the following apply to you:
- You carry on a trade or business as a sole proprietor or an independent contractor.
- You are a member of a partnership that carries on a trade or business.
- You are otherwise in business for yourself.

Trade or business. A trade or business is generally an activity carried on for a livelihood or in good faith to make a profit. The facts and circumstances of each case determine whether or not an activity is a trade or business. The regularity of activities and transactions and the production of income are important elements. You do not need to actually make a profit to be in a trade or business as long as you have a profit motive. You do need, however, to make ongoing efforts to further the interests of your business.

Part-time business. You do not have to carry on regular full-time business activities to be self-employed. Having a part-time business in addition to your regular job or business also may be self-employment.

Example. You are employed full time as an engineer at the local plant. You fix televisions and radios during the weekends. You have your own shop, equipment, and tools. You get your customers from advertising and word-of-mouth. You are self-employed as the owner of a part-time repair shop.

Sole proprietor. You are a sole proprietor if you own an unincorporated business by yourself, in most cases. However, if you are the sole member of a domestic limited liability company (LLC), you are not a sole proprietor if you elect to treat the LLC as a corporation. For more information on this election and the tax treatment of a foreign LLC, see Form 8832, Entity Classification Election. **www.irs.gov**

Intellectual Property

Lawful protection of intellectual property - consisting of business strategies, images, concepts and ideas - is often worth more to a business than its tangible assets.

www.Business.gov - Legal and regulatory information

Federal Copyrights - www.copyright.gov
Public Information Office 202-707-3000
Forms Hotline 202-707-9100
Copyright is a form of protection provided by the laws of the United States (Title 17, U.S. Code) to the authors of "original works of authorship", including literary, dramatic, musical, artistic, and certain other intellectual works. This protection is available to both published and unpublished works.

Federal Patents
A patent is an exclusive property right to an invention and is issued by the Commissioner of Patents and Trademarks, U.S. Department of Commerce. It gives an inventor the right to exclude others from making, using, or selling an invention for a period of 17 years in the United States, its territories, and possessions.

U.S. Patents and Trademark Office - www.uspto.gov
Patent & Trademark Office
Arlington, VA
703-308-4357 or 1-800-786-9199

Sirti
www.sirti.org
665 N. Riverpoint Blvd, Spokane, WA 99202-1665
509-358-2000
Sirti accelerates start-up and high-growth technology companies. Its state-of-the-art incubator facilities, seasoned entrepreneurial coaching and comprehensive client services, access to capital and access to legal services needed for Inland NW client companies' successful formation, IP protection and long-term success. Emphasis is given to energy, digital, and emerging technologies.

Federal Trademarks - www.uspto.gov
"Brand name" is a synonym for "trademark". Trademarks distinguish one firm's cornflakes or four-wheel-drive station wagons from another's. Without them, consumers could not buy products they like or avoid those they don't like. Trademarks may be words, logos or other symbols. Trademarks are not copyrights or patents. They cannot be used to prevent one firm from copying the goods or services of another, nor from selling its goods or services under a common descriptive (or generic) name.

Statewide Trademark Registration

State of Washington - Office of Secretary of State
www.sos.wa.gov/corps
360-753-7115; corps@secstate.wa.gov
Office of the Secretary of State
Corporate Division - Dolliver Building
801 Capital Way S., Olympia, WA 98504-0234
Monday - Friday, 8 am to 4 pm

Statewide Trademark Registration Idaho Secretary of State – Trademark Division
www.sos.idaho.gov
PO Box 83720, Boise ID 83720-0800
208-332-2810

Franchising

SBA Guidance for Franchisees - www.sba.gov
Download and use SBA's "Is Franchising for Me?"

SBA's Franchise Registry - www.franchiseregistry.com
A listing of franchise companies whose franchisees benefit from a streamlined review process for SBA loan applications.

The **10 most popular franchise industries** are fast food, retail, service, automotive, restaurants, maintenance, building and construction, business services, and lodging.

What is Franchising?
A franchise is a legal and commercial relationship between the owner of a trademark, service mark, trade name, or advertising symbol and an individual or group wishing to use that identification in a business. A franchisee conforms to the franchisor's business concept and sells goods or services supplied by the franchisor or that meet the franchisor's quality standards.

In the simplest form – product/trade name franchising - a franchiser owns the right to the name or trademark and sells that right to a franchisee. *The more complex form* - business format franchising - involves a broader ongoing relationship between the two parties. Business format franchises often provide a full range of services, including site selection, training, product supply, marketing plans, and even assistance in obtaining financing. Before selecting a franchise, consider your investment, your abilities and your goals.

Franchising Strategy - Closely evaluate the strength of the franchiser; the franchiser's long-term goal; the uniqueness of its product or service; the type of consumer response the product or service is achieving; the amount of fees it charges; the type of support it provides: 1) startup 2) operations 3) marketing; and the length of the contract you will be signing.

Pre-Purchase Detective Work - Investigate prior to any business purchase. Contact other franchisees. Obtain a uniform offering circular to understand vital details about the franchise's legal, financial, and personnel history before signing a contract.

Reasonable Expectations - Before signing, make sure that you will have the right to use the franchise name and trademark, receive training and management assistance from the franchisor, use the franchisor's expertise in marketing, advertising, facility design, layouts, displays, and fixtures, and do business in an area protected from other competing franchisees.

Some franchisees negotiate to have the franchisor help obtain building permits; purchase or lease equipment, signs and supplies; and construct or remodel the business premises.

Possible Pitfalls - The contract usually benefits the franchiser more than the franchisee. The franchisee is generally subject to sales quotas and often is required to purchase equipment, supplies, and inventory exclusively from the franchisor. The franchisor often has the right to terminate the franchise if it fails to operate the business according to the agreement, becomes delinquent on royalties, or violates other contract specifications.

Get Professional Help - Franchise tax rules are complex. Consult an attorney, preferably a specialist in franchise law, for assistance in evaluating the franchise package and tax considerations. An accountant can help to determine the full costs of purchasing and operating the business as well as the potential profit to the franchisee.

Franchising is a viable alternative to circumvent higher risks associated with starting a new, independent business from scratch. One out of every three dollars spent by Americans for goods and services is spent in a franchised business, per the International Franchising Association **www.franchise.org.**

Business Insurance

Buying business insurance is among the best ways to prepare for the unexpected. Without proper protection, misfortunes such as the death of a partner or key employee, embezzlement, a lawsuit, or a natural disaster could spell the end of a thriving operation

Ranging from indispensable worker's compensation insurance to the relatively obscure executive kidnapping coverage, insurance is available for nearly any business risk. Considering the multitude of options, carefully weigh whether the cost of certain premiums will justify the coverage for a given risk.

Types of Business Insurance to Consider

Automobile - A vehicle owned by your business should be insured for both liability and replacement purposes. But you may need special insurance (called "non-owned automobile coverage") for employees who use their own autos in your business. This policy covers the business' liability for any damage which may result from such usage. Some personal auto policies exclude business use. Contact your current agent to see if a commercial policy is needed.

Business Interruption Insurance - While property insurance may pay enough to replace damaged or destroyed equipment or buildings, how will you pay costs such as taxes, utilities and other continuation expenses during the period between when the damage occurs and when the property is replaced? Business interruption (or "business income") insurance can provide sufficient funds to pay your fixed expenses during a period of time when your business is not operational due to a covered loss.

Criminal Insurance – Despite heightened workplace security, theft and malicious damage are always possibilities. Dangers associated with hacking, vandalism, and general theft are obvious, but employee embezzlement is more common than most business owners think. Criminal insurance and employee bonds can provide protection against losses in most criminal areas.

D&O ("Director and Officer") Insurance - Under certain circumstances, officers and directors of a corporation may become personally liable for their actions on behalf of the company. This type of policy covers this liability.

General Liability - General liability insurance covers legal hassles due to claims of negligence. These help protect against payments as the result of bodily injury or property damage, medical expenses, the cost of defending lawsuits, and settlement bonds or judgments required during an appeal procedure.

Home-Based Business Insurance - Contrary to popular belief, standard homeowners' insurance policies do not automatically cover home-based business losses. Commonly needed insurance areas for home-based businesses include business property/office equipment, professional liability, personal and advertising injury, loss of business data, crime and theft, and disability. Contact your homeowners' insurance company to update your policy.

Internet Business Insurance - Web-based businesses may wish to look into specialized insurance that covers liability for damage done by hackers and viruses. In addition, e-insurance often covers specialized online activities, including lawsuits resulting from meta tag abuse, banner advertising, or electronic copyright infringement.

Key Person ("Key Man") Insurance – A company's business continuation plan outlines how the firm will maintain operations if a key person dies, falls ill, or leaves, but if you (and/or any other business partner or essential employee) are so critical to the operation of your business that it cannot continue in the event of your illness or death, you should consider "key man" insurance. Frequently required by banks or government loan programs, this coverage is usually life insurance that names the company as a beneficiary if an essential person dies or is disabled.

Malpractice Insurance/E&O - Some licensed professionals need protection against the cost of lawsuits/claims alleging that one's negligence or inappropriate action resulted in bodily injury or property damage; medical expenses; the cost of defending lawsuits, investigations and settlements; and bonds or judgments required during an appeal procedure.

Product Liability - Every product is capable of personal injury or property damage. Companies that manufacture, wholesale, distribute, and retail a product may be liable for its safety. Additionally, every service rendered may be capable of personal injury or property damage. Businesses are considered liable for negligence, breach of an express or implied warranty, defective products, and defective warnings or instructions.

Worker's Compensation - Required in every state except Texas, worker's compensation insurance pays for employees' medical expenses and missed wages. In most cases, business owners, independent contractors, domestic employees in private homes, farm workers, and unpaid volunteers are exempt.

Do you need a Business Plan? Yes!

....a business plan gives you a path to follow. It can help make the future what you want it to be, with goals and action steps to guide your business through turbulent economic cycles.

....a business plan lets your banker in on the action. By reading the details of your business plan, your lender gains insight into your situation that will help determine whether or not to lend you money.

....a business plan provides a way to communicate your operations, goals, and business philosophy to personnel, suppliers and your other business contacts.

....a business plan develops you as a manager by making you construct a clear "blueprint" of your business venture.

Start with the Basics

While there are many good business plan formats, this one has been used successfully by thousands of small business owners. Feel free to modify the format to suit your needs.

☐ Executive Summary

Summarize your plan in two pages or less. Make it enthusiastic, professional, complete and concise. Include the goals and objectives of the business. If applying for a loan, state the amount desired.

If you had five minutes to explain the basics of your business to an investor, what would you say? That is what goes in the summary. Write this section last.

☐ Company Description

Give a brief company history.
What does your company do? What are your products?
Who are your customers? Where are you located?
What are your key strengths? Is your industry or market growing?
Who are the owners?
Is the firm a proprietorship, partnership, or corporation?

☐ Products and Services

What are your products (or services)?
Price and quality levels?
Distribution channels (i.e., how are products moved to the customers)?
Major competitors?
What makes your products particularly attractive?

☐ Marketing

(NOTE: In this section, be as specific as possible. Use statistics and numbers, and note your sources. Too many marketing plans are just enthusiastic fluff).

■ Product
Describe your product or service from your customer's point of view.
What do customers l ke and disl ke about your products, services, and company?
Why do they patronize you?
What services are offered as part of the product (delivery, service, warranty, support, refund offers)?

■ Economics
What are the characteristics of your industry. growing, declining, changing?
What is the size of your market?
What is your share of the market?
Is it growing? What is the demand for your product?
Are more firms entering? What are the barriers to entry?
Is it becoming more competitive; are profits being squeezed?

■ Customers
Identify your customers, their characteristics, their location.
Why will they patronize you?
What do they like about your company?

■ Competition
List your major competitors.
Describe their size, location, reputations.
Compare your goods and services with theirs.
What are their major advantages?
What are yours?

■ Strategy
What is your pricing policy? Why?
How do you promote, advertise, and sell?
How do you distr bute or deliver your products/services?
What customer services will you offer?
Relate your strategy to prior discussions of Product, Economics, Customers, and Competition.

☐ Sales Forecast

Now that you have written a description of your market, you need to do a detailed forecast of sales, by department, month by month, for the coming year.

☐ Operations Plan

■ Production
Methods of production, product development, quality control, inventory control.

■ Location.
Describe the physical location and explain why it is appropriate.
Is it leased or owned?

■ Credit Policies
Do you sell in credit? What terms? How do you check credit?
Collection policies?

■ Personnel
Number and type of employees.
Pay and personnel policies.
Do you have position descriptions and training programs?

■ Inventory
How much? What is its value?
List major suppliers.
Do they extend credit?
Who pays freight?
Do they give discounts?

■ Legal Environment
Licensing, bonding, permits, insurance, zoning, government regulations, patents, trademarks, copyrights.

☐ Management and Organization

Who has management responsibilities?
Resumes of all key managers.
Position descriptions for key employees. List important advisors, such as attorney, accountant, banker, insurance agent, and advisory board or board of directors, if you have one.

☐ Personal Financial Statements

Include personal financial statements of all owners and major stockholders.

☐ Startup Expenses and Capital

Carefully research your startup expenses: keep notes to document your numbers, organize your figures by dividing startup expenses into major categories. We suggest:

Buildings/Real Estate - Leasehold Improvements
Capital Equipment - Location & Admin. Expenses
Advertising & Promotion - Opening Inventory
Other Expenses - Contingencies - Working Capital

The contingency category is a way of allowing for costs which cannot be foreseen no matter how thorough your planning. Experienced entrepreneurs suggest you add 15% to 20% to your estimated expenses to allow for them.

Working capital is money needed to operate and pay bills while the business gets going. A carefully planned cash flow projection is the only good way to estimate working capital needs. Starting without adequate working capital will ensure early failure of the business.

If this is a startup, you must also show the sources of capital. Sources could include you, your partners or investors, private lenders, your bank, and perhaps equipment leases.

☐ Financial History

If your firm is established, include financial statements for at least the past three years as an appendix to the plan.

Our computer template includes a spreadsheet on which these historical statements can be condensed and laid out side by side for comparison. It is a good idea to include some key ratios in addition to the raw numbers. Current ratio, debt to net worth, return on equity, and Inventory turnover are a few useful basic ratios.

Include an aging of accounts receivable, showing the total amount owing you from customers, and how much is current, 30 days past due, 60 days, 90 days, and over 90 days past due.

Do the same for accounts payable.

☐ Projected Balance Sheet

Your plan should include a projected balance sheet showing assets (things owned), liabilities (debts), and owner's equity. If yours is a startup business, the balance sheet should show your financial position on opening day. Existing firms should do a projected year-end balance sheet.

If you are using the business plan to apply for a loan, prepare a pro-forma balance sheet projecting your financial position as of the day after the loan.

☐ 12-Month Profit Projection

In many ways, this is the capstone of your whole business plan. This is where it all comes together, where you show in detail how your company will make a profit.

Start by projecting sales month by month for the coming year. Break monthly sales into categories or departments; for example: by product type, customer group, geographic territory, or different contracts or projects. A projection built up in this fashion will be more accurate than just guessing total sales for the month. Your Marketing Plan should be the basis for these projections.

Now estimate the Cost of Goods Sold (COGS) for each category of sales for each month. COGS are those expenses directly related to producing or purchasing the product/service you sell.

For retailers, COGS is the cost of buying merchandise; for manufacturers and construction, it is direct production labor and materials. For services businesses, it is production labor and materials. Breaking COGS down into departments will help you see which parts of the business deliver the most profit per sales dollar.

Now estimate operating expenses month by month for the year. These are necessary expenses which are *not* directly related to buying or making your product/service. They are also known as overhead items. Examples are: telephone, rent, insurance, taxes, and the salaries of office, sales, and management personnel. Use the same categories of expense you use (or plan to use) in the regular Income Statements you get from your accountant. This makes it easier to draw on history in making projections, and it makes it easier to compare your actual statements to your plan as time goes by.

☐ Cash Flow Projection

Your profit projection will show how you intend to prosper by having revenues exceed expenses. Now you must show that you can pay your bills while prospering. Bills are paid with cash, not with profits.

A cash flow projection is basically nothing more than a forward look at your checking account. It is derived from the profit projection, but looks at the financial data in slightly different ways. The fundamental differences are:

■ On the income side, a cash flow asks not when a sale is made, but rather when cash is actually collected from the customer.

■ On the outgo side, the question is not when an expense is incurred, but rather when the check will have to be written to pay the bill.

■ Some items show only on one of the two statements, but not on the other. Depreciation, for example is a real business expense, but not an item of cash flow (you never write a check for depreciation). On the other hand, the principle part of a loan repayment is not an expense (only the interest portion is), but it definitely takes cash out of the business, and therefore needs to be shown on the cash flow projection.

By forecasting the status of your bank account, the Cash Flow tells you whether your working capital reserves are adequate. Budgeting does not create sales or put money in the bank, but it can help put you in control. When you know how much the off season will draw down your account, and how much it will take to get started on that new contract, and when you begin negotiating that new bank loan months in advance because you can foresee the need, then you have gained a little more control over your own destiny.

All your projections should be based on careful research, not casual guesswork. Keep notes detailing your major assumptions and attach the notes to your projections.

Free Business Plan Templates
www.score.org - click on "Templates and Tools"

Free Business Plan Workshop
app1.sba.gov/training/sbabp

SCORE

For any start-up or existing small business, SCORE volunteers provide confidential and free one-on-one or team counseling. For counseling, training, business tips and free templates contact your local SCORE office. **www.score.org**

Western Washington

Seattle Chapter #55
www.seattlescore.org
2401 Fourth Avenue, Suite 450
Seattle, WA 98121-3419
206-553-7320 or 1-877-732-7267
On-site counseling and workshops
Monday - Friday, 9 am to 4 pm

Bainbridge Island Chamber	206-842-4162
Bellevue Library	425-450-1760
Bothell L brary	425-344-4071
Bremerton Chamber	360-479-3579
Coupeville	888-506-7999
Everett L brary	425-257-8000
Friday Harbor	360-378-2906
Kirkland Library	425-822-2459
Kitsap Business Asst Center	360-307-4220
Mercer Island L brary	206-236-3537
Mount Vernon	360-416-7873
Mukilteo WBC	425-954-4040
EDC/Port Angeles	360-457-7793
Redmond Chamber	425-647-8312
Shoreline Library	206-362-7550
Silverdale Chamber	360-692-6800
Woodinville	425-821-9780

Bellingham Chapter #591
www.scorechapter591.org
Bellingham: 360-685-4259
Coupeville: 888-506-7999

Olympia Branch
www.thurstonedc.com
click on "Business Resources"
665 Woodland Square Loop SE, Suite 201
Lacy, WA 98503
360-754-6320

Tacoma Chapter #385
co-located at Bates Technical College
1101 S. Yakima, Room M-123B
Tacoma, WA 98405
253-680-7770

Eastern Washington

Central Washington Chapter #663
www.centralwashingtonSCORE.org
Wenatchee: 509-662-2116
Ephrata: 509-754-4656
Lake Chelan: 509-682-3503
Leavenworth: 509-548-5807
Moses Lake: 509-765-7888
Omak: 509-826-1880
Quincy: 509-787-2140
Waterville: 509-745-8871

Mid-Columbia Chapter #590
Kennewick: 509-736-0510
Pasco: 509-547-9755
Richland: 509-946-1651
Richland: 509-372-7142
West Richland: 509-967-0521

Spokane Chapter #180
www.scorespokane.org
Spokane: 509-353-2821
Colville: 800-776-7318
Spokane Valley: 509-924-4994

Yakima Valley Chapter #664
http://yakimascore.org/
Yakima: 509-248-2021
Ellensburg: 509-933-1847; score@paktec.com

Northern Idaho
Moscow: SteveB@moscow.com
Post Falls: 208-777-3151
Sandpoint: 208-263-4073

"Be patient and honest with yourself and do your homework.
Go into business for the love of it.
Remember, customers make a company successful."

Raci Erdem, White House Grill
Post Falls, Idaho
SBDC counseling & SBA loan recipient

Women Biz Resources

Women's Business Centers
Provide technical training, counseling and financing options

NW Women's Business Center
www.nwwbc.org
425-423-9090
infonwwbc@seattleccd.com

South Sound Women's Business Center
co-located at Bates Technical College
http://sswbc.seattleccd.com/
253-680-7194
Cloverpark Technical College
253-589-4523

Washington Business Center
http://wbc.seattleccd.com/
206-324-4330

Women's Network for Entrepreneurial Training WNET
At every stage of developing and expanding your business, WNET is here to teach, encourage and inspire. WNET provides dynamic networking and interactive training sessions for both men and women.

WNET Training Schedule
www.sba.gov/wa
Fresh business management topics are lead by dedicated business owners and experts who can help you start, grow and succeed.

WA Office of Minority and Women's Business Enterprises - OMWBE
www.omwbe.wa.gov
Provides certification to increase participation of minority and women's businesses to state public works contracting, purchasing of goods and services, and loans.

National Association of Women Business Owners (NAWBO) Inland Northwest Chapter
www.nawbonw.org
Spokane, info@nawbonw.org
Network of women business owners who share ideas, learn, and expand opportunities for all women business owners.

www.womenbiz.gov
Government contracts can be a great source of business revenue for both new and established businesses. Find helpful links and information for women-owned businesses selling to the federal government.

Small Business Development Centers

Certified Business Advisors deliver professional one-on-one business counseling, quality training classes, and research services for existing small business throughout Washington State and Northern Idaho.

More information is online at **www.wsbdc.org** (Washington) or **www.idahosbdc.org** (Idaho)

Washington State SBDC Lead Office
www.wsbdc.org
Washington State University
534 E. Spokane Falls Blvd, Spokane, WA 99210-1495
Brett Rogers, State Director
Duane Fladland, Associate State Director
509-358-7765, sbdc@wsu.edu

Idaho State SBDC Lead Office
www.idahosbdc.org
Boise State University
1021 Manitou Avenue, Boise, ID 83725-1655
James Hogge, State Director
208-426-3799; 1-800-225-3815

Idaho

Lewiston, ID: Lewis-Clark State College
VACANT/Judy Schumacher, 208-792-2465; schumacher@lcsc.edu

Post Falls, ID: Workforce Training Center
William Jhung, 208-666-8009; william_jhung@nic.edu

Washington

Aberdeen: WSU/Grays Harbor Community College
Er k Stewart, 360-538-2530; eriks@wsu.edu

Auburn: Green River Community College
Deanna Burnett-Keener, 253-333-4953; dburnett@greenriver.edu

Bellingham: Western Washington University
Jennifer Shelton, 360-778-1762; Jennifer.shelton@wwu.edu

Bremerton: WSU
Elaine Jones, 360-307-4220; elaine.jones@wsbdc.org

Chehalis: Lewis County EDC
David Baria, 360-748-0114; dbaria@lewisedc.com

Des Moines: Highline Community College
Zev Siegl, 206-878-3710, ext 5151; sbdc@highline.edu
Rich Shockley, 206-878-3710, ext 5150; rshockley@highline.edu

Everett: Edmonds Community College
Peter Quist, 425-640-1435; peter.quist@edcc.edu

Kent: Green River Community College
Kirk Davis, 253-520-6262; kdavis@greenriver.edu

Longview: WSU
Vacant/Buck Heidrick, 360-442-2946; buck.heidrick@wsbdc.org

Mt. Vernon: EDA of Skagit Valley
Dean Shellan, 360-336-6114; dean@skagit.org

Moses Lake: WSU
Allan Peterson, 509-762-2373; allanp@bigbend.edu

Okanogan: Economic Alliance of Okanogan County
Lew Blakeney, 509-826-5107; blakeney@methow.com

Olympia: South Puget Sound Community College
Ron Nielsen, 360-407-0014; rnielsen@spscc.ctc.edu

Port Angeles: WSU/Clallam County EDC
Kathleen Purdy, Washington State University
360-417-5657; kpurdy@olympus.net

Port Townsend: WSU/Jefferson County EDC
Kathleen Purdy, Washington State University
360-344-3078; kpurdy@olympus.net

Pullman: WSU
Terry Cornelison, 509-335-8081; tlcornelison@wsu.edu

Renton: WSU/Renton Technical College
Asbury Lockett, 425-235-7819; asbury.lockett@wsbdc.org

Seattle: WSU West
Michael Franz, 206-428-3022; mfranz@wsu.edu

Seattle: WSU/Evergreen Business Capital
Steve Burke, 206-246-4445; steve.burke@wsbdc.org

Spokane: WSU
Alan Stanford, 509-358-7890 or 7892; alan.stanford@wsu.edu
Dennis Hake, 509-358-7890 or 7893; dennis.hake@wsbdc.org

Tacoma: WSU/Bates Technical College
John Rodenberg, 253-680-7768; jrodenberg@bates.ctc.edu

Tri-Cities: TRIDEC/Columbia Basin College
Bruce Davis, 509-735-6222; bdavis@columbiabasin.edu

Vancouver: WSU
Janet Harte, 360-260-6372; jharte@vancouver.wsu.edu
Buck Heidrick, 360-442-2946; buck.heidrick@wsbdc.org

Wenatchee: WSU/Port of Chelan
Jim Fletcher, 509-888-7252; jim.fletcher@wsbdc.org

Yakima: WSU/Yakima Chamber of Commerce
Linda Johnson; 509-454-7612; linda@yakima.org

Hispanic Outreach
Skagit/Mt. Vernon
Diana Morell, 360-336-6114; diana@skagit.org

Everett
Jose Garcia-Pabon
425-338-2400; garciajl@wsu.edu

International Trade - Export Readiness Centers
Terry Chambers, IT Director, Spokane
509-358-7894; terryc@wsu.edu

Seattle: WSU/Evergreen Business Capital
Joseph Vogel, 206-246-5341; joseph.vogel@wsbdc.org
Stan Lance, 206-439-3785; stan.lance@wbsdc.org

Spokane: WSU
Vern Jenkins, 509-358-7998; vern.jenkins@wsbdc.org
Katerina Korish, 509- 358-7593; katerina.korish@wsbdc.org

The SBA Loan Guarantee Program: How it Works
www.sba.gov/financialassistance

The SBA helps small businesses obtain needed credit by giving the government's guaranty to loans made by commercial lenders. The lender makes the loan and SBA will repay up to 85% of any loss in case of default. Since this is a bank loan, applications are submitted to the bank and loan payments are paid to the bank. The bank is also responsible for closing the loan and disbursing the loan proceeds. Most commercial banks and some non-bank commercial lenders participate in this program.

SBA's involvement is limited to reviewing the loan application submitted by the bank to assure they meet eligibility and credit standards. SBA provides the bank with a written Authorization outlining the conditions of the SBA guarantee; any material changes to this authorization generally require SBA approval.

Find the SBA Participating Lender List at www.sba.gov/wa under "Resources"

The **7(a) guaranteed loan program** is SBA's primary lending program.

The borrower applies to a lending institution, not the SBA. The lender applies to the SBA for a loan guaranty. The SBA can process the lender's request through a variety of methods. Guarantees are up to $3,750,000 of each loan made by participant lenders.

These loans typically range from $25,000 to $5 million and are repaid in monthly installments. They can be used for a variety of business purposes including working capital, equipment acquisition, debt refinance, change of ownership, and real estate purchases. Maturities depend on the use of loan proceeds but typically range from 5 to 25 years.

Streamlined 7(a) Loan Processing

Preferred Lender program - SBA has delegated certain lenders the authority to approve SBA loans unilaterally. Preferred lenders operate under the same 7(a) guaranteed loan guidelines as detailed above. SBA generally provides a loan guarantee to the lender within 24 hours of their request.

SBA Express Loan Program - SBAExpress loans are backed by an SBA guarantee of 50 percent, the lender uses its own application and documentation forms and the lender has unilateral credit approval authority as in the PLP Program. This method makes it easier and faster for lenders to provide small business loans of $350,000 or less, with SBA generally providing a loan guarantee to the lender within 24 hours of their request.

Patriot Express Loans - Loans of up to $500,000 are available to veterans and members of the military community. Eligible military community members include: Veterans and Service-disabled veterans; Active-duty service members eligible for the military's Transition Assistance Program; Reservists and National Guard members; current spouses of any of the above; and the widowed spouse of a service member or veteran who died during service or of a service-connected disability.

Loans can be used for most business purposes, including start-up, expansion, equipment purchases, working capital, inventory or business-occupied real-estate purchases. They qualify for SBA's maximum guaranty of up to 85% for loans of $150,000 or less, and up to 75% for loans over $150,000 up to $500,000. Patriot Express loans feature SBA's fastest turnaround time for loan approvals, and lowest interest rates for business loans - generally 2.25 percent to 4.75 percent over prime depending upon the size and maturity of the loan.

General Credit Requirements

SBA and private lenders use similar criteria to test credit worthiness.
(1) Repayment Ability: You must show that you can meet business expenses, owners draw, and loan payments from the earnings of the business. This is demonstrated through historical performance and/or thoroughly documented cash flow projections.
(2) Management: You must show ability to operate the business successfully. For a start-up, you should have experience in the type of business you propose to start, as well as some significant work experience at a management level.
(3) Equity: The owners must have enough of their own money at stake in the business:
    (a) *For a New Business* (or when buying a business) you should have approximately one dollar of cash or business assets for each three dollars of the loan.
    (b) *For an Established Firm,* the after-the-loan business balance sheet should show no more than four dollars of total debt for each dollar of net worth (i.e., a 4:1 Debt/Equity ratio, although this may vary by industry).

Definition of Equity: You may be required to pledge nonbusiness assets (often a second mortgage on your personal residence may be required for collateral). However, this should not be confused with equity in the sense it is used here. As used here, the equity is the owner's net investment in the business.

(4) Credit History: Your personal and company credit histories will be reviewed. Prudent lenders prefer applicants who have a history of meeting their obligations. If your credit record has blemishes but there are extenuating circumstances, prepare to explain fully.

Guarantee Portion - Under the 7(a) guaranteed loan program SBA typically guarantees from 50% to 85% of an eligible bank loan up to a maximum guaranty amount of $,750,000. The exact percentage of the guaranty depends on a variety of factors such as size of loan and which SBA program is to be used. This will be worked out between the SBA and your bank.

Amounts - The maximum loan amount is $5 million. The total SBA guarantee for any one borrower may not exceed $3,750,000.

Maturity - Up to 25 years for real estate acquisition or construction. Most other SBA loans are limited to 10 years. Working capital loans are generally limited to seven years.

Interest Rates - SBA sets a maximum rate on its guaranteed loans. The rate may be either fixed or variable, as determined between the lender and applicant. The rate is pegged to the prime rate as published daily in the Wall Street Journal. The formulas are:
- Prime + 2.25% for loans > $50,000, maturity < 7 years.
- Prime + 2.75% for loans > $50,000, maturity 7 years or more.
- Lenders have the option of charging an additional 1% on loans under $50,000 and 2% on loans under $25,000.

Fees

SBA charges a fee for its guaranty. The fee is levied on that portion of the loan guaranteed by SBA, not the face amount of the loan. It is passed along to the borrower and is usually financed - i.e., built into the loan amount.

Fees for loan maturity exceeding 12 months:
- 2% of the guaranteed portion for loans up to $150,000
- 3% of the guaranteed portion for loans above $150,000 up to $700,000
- 3.5% of the guaranteed portion for loans above $700,000
- An additional .25% fee is charged on guaranteed amounts in excess of $1 million.

Fees for loan maturity of 12 months or less:
- .25% (1/4 of 1%) of the guaranteed portion

Prepayment Penalties - Only on loans with terms of 15 years or longer. Decreasing prepayment penalties apply during the first three years of the loan.

Collateral - SBA's policy has two parts:
(1) When a loan guaranty is approved, we expect all available company assets to be offered as collateral. If company assets are insufficient to fully secure the loan, liens on personal assets may be required. Often, this means a lien on residential real estate.

(2) On the other hand, if adequate collateral simply is not available, this fact alone will not cause SBA to decline an otherwise qualified loan.

Eligibility - Most small businesses are eligble to receive SBA loan guarantees, however ineligible applicant cases include:

1. The applicant is not small business.
2. The funds are otherwise available on reasonable terms, e.g., if the bank would make the same loan terms available without an SBA guaranty, or if personal assets could be used without hardship to the owners.
3. The loan is to pay off inadequately secured creditors.
4. Your business is engaged in speculation, lending, investment, or rental real estate.
5. The applicant is a nonprofit enterprise (except employee stock ownership programs).

Size Standards - Applicants must meet the SBA definition of small business. Size limits vary by specific industry (NAICS code). See page 20 or **www.sba.gov/size**.

Additional SBA Financing Programs

Export Working Capital - www.buyusa.gov/seattle/sba.html
Export Assistance Center, 206-553-0051
Loans used to finance export sales 90% SBA guaranty up to $1.5 million.

Microloan Programs
Increases the availability of small scale financing and technical assistance to prospective small business borrowers.
Loans range from $500 to $50,000.

SBA Designated Microloan Lenders:
Seattle: Community Capital Development, 206-324-4330
Seattle: Washington CASH, 206-352-1945
Richland: Benton-Franklin Council of Gov't, 509-943-9185
Spokane: SNAP Financial Access, 509-456-7174 x 111
Yakima: Rural Community Dev Resources, 509-453-5133

Hayden, ID: Panhandle Area Council, 208-772-0584

504 Certified Development Company (CDC) Loan Program
http://www.sba.gov/content/cdc504-loan-program
A CDC is a nonprofit corporation set up to contribute to the economic development of its community or region. They work with the SBA and private-sector lenders to provide long term, fixed rate financing for the acquisition or improvement of owner occupied commercial buildings as well as for major equipment purchases.

504 is a partnership financing arrangement with a first mortgage lender typically funding 50% of an eligible project. SBA funds 40% and the small business typically contr butes 10%.

SBA's 504 loan amount is usually capped at $5 million, whole amount actually can borrower up to 5.5 million

Ameritrust CDC, 206-402-3971
Evergreen Business Capital, 206-622-3731
NWBDA, 509-458-8555
Panhandle Area Council, 208-772-0584

SBA Disaster Loans
www.sba.gov/services/disasterassistance
Field Operations West, 800-488-5323

If you are in a declared disaster area and are the victim of a disaster, you may be eligible for an SBA Disaster Loan - even if you don't own a business. As a homeowner, renter and/or personal-property owner, you may apply to the SBA for a loan to help you recover from a disaster.

Physical Disaster Loans: Available for non-farm businesses of any size and non-profit organizations. SBA makes loans of up to $1.5 million to repair or replace damaged property, inventory, and equipment.

Economic Injury Disaster Loans: Small businesses or agricultural cooperatives may be eligible for SBA assistance of up to $1.5 million if they have suffered substantial economic injury in a declared disaster area.

Real Property Loans: Loans up to $200,000 for homeowners to repair or restore a primary residence to its previous condition.

Personal Property Loans: Up to $40,000 for homeowners and renters to repair or replace personal property such as clothing, furniture, or automobiles lost in the disaster.

Interest Rates: By law, rates are not to exceed 4% for homeowners, renters and businesses unable to obtain credit elsewhere. Rates are not to exceed 8 percent for homeowners, renters and businesses determined by SBA to have credit available elsewhere.

Federal Emergency Management Agency
Homeowners and renters must register with FEMA to obtain a FEMA ID number.

Call FEMA at **1-800-621-3362** or (TTY) 1-800-462-7585

SBA disaster questions?

Call **1-800-659- 2955** or (TTY)1-800-877-8339
Email **disastercustomerservice@sba.gov**

SBA Loan FAQs

Does the SBA provide grants to start or expand small businesses?

No. The SBA *does not* offer direct grants of money for starting or expanding the operations of a small business. SBA's grant programs generally support nonprofit organizations, intermediary lending institutions, and state and local governments in an effort to expand and enhance small business technical and financial assistance.

There are grants available to small businesses through various federal agencies, however, these grants are typically awarded to existing businesses and are narrow in purpose, such as the Small Business Innovation Research Program **www.sba.gov/SBIR** which awards grants to established and qualified enterprises to develop new technologies. You can obtain more information on grants offered by various federal, state and local organizations at **www.grants.gov**.

Do I need to be declined by a bank before applying for an SBA loan guaranty?

No. The SBA helps small businesses obtain needed credit by giving the government's guaranty to loans made by commercial lenders. The lender makes the loan, and SBA promises to repay up to 85% of any loss in case of default. Most commercial banks and some nonbank commercial lenders participate in this program.

Does my business qualify for SBA assistance?

Approximately 98% of all businesses are eligible for SBA help. Ineligible businesses include those described on *page 13 under Eligibility*.

What can I do to increase my chances of getting a loan?

Research and develop a business plan that includes realistic financial projections and an estimate of anticipated earnings. A well planned and organized business plan will be an important factor when a lending officer reviews your request. See Writing a Business plan on *page 10*.

How much personal investment or contribution do I need to qualify for a loan?

If you're a start-up, you can typically expect to provide approximately 20 to 30 percent of the total required starting capital. If you're an established business, the ratio of total debt-to-net worth after the loan is made should be approximately 4:1 or better in most cases.

What is the turnaround time for a loan to be processed?

If all the loan documentation is complete, a preferred lender can get an SBA approval within 24 hours of submitting the documents to SBA; a certified lender can get SBA approval in as few as three days.

What is the Preferred Lender Program (PLP)?

The PLP maximizes the use of qualified lenders. SBA delegates loan approval, closing, and most servicing and liquidation authority and responsibility to carefully selected lenders. Other non-PLP lenders can submit applications under the traditional method, where the SBA reviews the lender's credit analysis and examines eligibility.

Where can I obtain a loan application?

Application forms and procedures differ depending on the lender. For example some lenders may have you complete a paper loan application while others offer an on-line application. If the lender determines that an SBA guarantee is required, they will work with you to complete certain SBA forms. SBA loan forms are availble from participating lenders or via download at **www.sba.gov/tools/forms/index.html**

If my loan application is declined, what other options do I have?

Don't give up. There may be other financial resources better suited for your needs. There are other financial entities that use different evaluative techniques and loan money at a slightly higher interest rate than a traditional bank loan. In addition, some states, counties, and cities commonly work with local banks to provide financial support to small businesses as part of their economic development programs. Ask your banker to help you explore these options. *Financing Options page 17.*

Financial Components of a Business Plan

New Business
(1) Describe in detail the type of business to be established.
(2) Describe your experience and management credentials.
(3) Prepare a detailed estimate of how much capital will be needed to start. State how much you have and how much you will need to borrow.
(4) Prepare a current personal financial statement, listing all personal assets and liabilities.
(5) Prepare a month-by-month projection of revenues, expenses and profit for the first twelve months. Also do a companion cash flow projection for the same period. Explain your major assumptions in an accompanying narrative.
(6) List the collateral to be offered as security for the loan, with estimates of the market value of each item.
(7) Take this material to your banker. If the bank wants an SBA guaranty for your loan, they will make application to us. You deal with the bank; the bank deals with SBA.

Established Business
(1) Current business financial information: Prepare a current balance sheet and an income (profit and loss) statement for current year up to the date of the balance sheet.
(2) Historical business financial information: Prepare income statements and balance sheets for the past three full years. Do not include personal items on the statements. Reconcile the equity balances between each year.
(3) Prepare a month-by-month projection of revenues, expenses and profits for the next twelve months. Also do a companion cash flow projection for the same period. Explain your major assumptions in an accompanying narrative.
(4) Prepare a current personal financial statement for each owner, partner, or stockholder owning at least 20% of the business.
(5) List the collateral to be offered as security for the loan, with estimates of the market value of each item.
(6) State the amount and intended uses of the loan.
(7) Take this material to your banker. If the bank wants an SBA guaranty for your loan, they will make application to us. You deal with the bank; the bank deals with SBA.

GRANTS

The SBA does NOT offer grants to start or expand small businesses. SBA does offer some grant programs, however they are designed to expand and enhance organizations that provide small business management, technical, or financial assistance. These grants generally support non-profit organizations, intermediary lending institutions, and state and local governments.

Catalog of Federal Domestic Assistance (CFDA) - www.cfda.gov

The on-line catalog covers a wide variety of Federal programs, projects, services, and activities which provide assistance or benefits to the American public. There are currently 15 types of assistance available including surplus equipment, training, guaranteed loans, and, of course, grants.

Federal Grant Resources
www.grants.gov
A listing of grants available through a variety of federal, state and local organizations. *The SBA does not provide grants for starting or expanding the operations of a business.*

FINANCING OPTIONS

SBA Certified Development Companies CDC

CDCs use public and private partnerships to finance fixed assets for small firms and plays a key role in creating and retaining jobs. Most 504 projects are in the $200,000 to $2 Million range.

Ameritrust
www.ameritrustcdc.com
1127 10th Ave E., Suite 1
Seattle, WA 98102
206-402-3971

Evergreen Business Capital
www.evergreen504.com
SBA 504 Loan Program
13925 Interurban Avenue S. Suite 100
Seattle, WA 98168
800-878-6613

NW Business Development Association
www.nwbusiness.org
Spokane 509-458-8555
9019 E. Appleway, Suite 200
Spokane Valley, WA 99212
Seattle 425-235-9917
15 S. Grady Way, Suite 517
Seattle, WA 98057

Panhandle Area Council (PAC)
www.pacni.org
11100 N. Airport Drive
Hayden, ID 83835
208-772-0584; paulferg@pacni.org
Serves the 5 northern counties of Idaho, and other business loan programs.

Alternative Financing

Benton Franklin Council of Governments
PO Box 217, Richland, WA 99352
509-943-9185
Nontraditional loan funds for gap financing in manufacturing, value-added processing, service and retail. It can be used for fixed assets, working capital, inventory and real estate. Funding for firms in **Benton, Franklin and Walla Walla counties**.

Center for Economic Opportunity (CEO)
15 N. Broadway, Ste B, Tacoma, WA 98403
253-591-7026
Assists TANF and low-income persons of **Pierce County** to pursue self employment as a means of achieving self-sufficiency. Teaches small business skills and provides access to capital.

Coastal Revolving Loan Fund
www.kitsapeda.org
Kitsap Economic Development Alliance
4312 Kitsap Way, Suite 103
Bremerton, WA 98312
360-479-3712
Low interest loans for start-up projects, expansion or purchase in areas affected by fishing and timber industry declines in **Clallam, Jefferson, Grays Harbor, Pacific or Wahkiakum** counties. Max $50,000.

Community Capital Development (CCD)
http://seattleccd.com/drupal
1437 South Jackson, Seattle, WA 98144
206-324-4330
Serves women, veterans and small businesses with general management/ marketing, financial planning analysis, and contract procurement assistance. *CCD also offers the SBA 7(a) and Microloan programs.*

Development Loan Fund (DLF)
Department of Community Development
906 Columbia Street SW
Olympia, WA 98504-8300
360-753-0325
Loans up to $350,000 for businesses in distressed **rural areas** to create new jobs, particularly for lower income persons.

Enterprise Cascadia
www.sbpac.com
401 2nd Ave. S., Seattle, WA 98104
206-447-9226
Provides loans and technical assistance to entrepreneurs unable to access traditional financing. Lends to women, minorities, and low-income people, and to businesses which restore or preserve the environment or have strong potential to create jobs. Loans range from $5,000 to $500,000.

Evergreen Business Capital Rural Loan Fund
www.evergreen504.com
800-878-6613
Loan program for rural WA businesses in towns with populations of 25,000 or less. Amounts from $10,000 - $250,000.

HAEIFC Private Business Loans
www.haeifc.com
509-539-6509, loans@haeifc.com
For for-profit firms in **Benton & Franklin counties.** Funds R&D, machinery/ equipment or land purchases, renovations, leasehold improvements, and/or construction-related costs. Loans may require owner capital injection. Minimum loan is $150,000. Maximum term is 20 years.

North Central Washington Business Loan Fund
www.ncwloanfund.org
410 E. Woodin Ave. P.O. Box 3032
Chelan, WA 98816
509-860-4330; ncwloanfund@nwi.net
Offers loans from $5,000 to $150,000 in **Okanogan, Chelan & Douglas Counties and the Colville Indian Reservation.**

Pierce County
Dept of Community Services
www.co.pierce.wa.us/PC/
3602 Pacific Avenue, Suite 200
Tacoma, WA 98418
Sheree Clark, 253-798-6604;
pcecondev@co.pierce.wa.us
Assist new and existing businesses. Funding sources include: HUD, SBA and the Pierce County Community Investment Corporation.

Quest Revolving Loan Fund
Columbia Station, 3rd Floor
300 S Columbia St., Wenatchee, WA 98801
509-663-5711
Covers **Chelan** and **Douglas** Counties. Existing businesses only. Also offers GAP financing with banks.

The Lending Network
1611 N. National Avenue
Chehalis, WA 98532
360-740-6960
tkalendnet@localaccess.com
Rural Development Loan fund serves **Lewis, Cowlitz and South Thurston counties** in Washington State. Loan amounts from $25,000 to $250,000; terms up to 20 years; fixed interest rates; collateral required; job creation requirement.

Washington Dept of Commerce (formerly Commerce, Trade & Economic Development - CTED)
www.commerce.wa.gov
Helps entrepreneurs obtain financing for start-up and expansion projects. Helps with business plan, finance and implement strategies for company and job growth. Its loan programs include Rural Washington Loan Fund, Forest Products Revolving Loan Fund, Child Care Facility Fund, Coastal Loan Fund, HUD Section 108 Guaranteed Loans, CDBG Float Loans, Brownfields Cleanup Revolving Fund.

WA State Linked Deposit Program
http://www.omwbe.wa.gov/financing/ldp/index.shtml
Seattle, 206-956-3165
For certified minority and women-owned businesses in WA. Loans at below market rate. See participating banks online.

WDVA Veterans Linked Deposit Program
www.dva.wa.gov/linked%20deposit.html
800-562-0132 Option 1
communications@dva.wa.gov
For certified Veteran-owned businesses in WA. Decreases loan nterest rates up to 2%. Participating bank list online. Loan limit $1 million, 10-year maximum term. Commercial financing for lines of credit, accounts receivables, working capital, equipment purchases, and real property aquisition.

MICROLOAN LENDERS

AHANA - African American, Hispanic, Asian & Native American
www.ahana.org
25 W. Main, Suite 300, Spokane WA 99201
509-209-2634; bcabildo@ahana.org
Loans up to $15,000 for working capital, expansion and/or start-ups at prime plus 2% fixed term. Need viable business plan.

BFCoG Regional Revolving Loans
www.bfcog.us
509-943-9185, atackett@bfcog.us
Gap financing for job-creating business expansion within **Benton and Franklin counties.** Gap loans beyond conventional financing range from $25,000 to $175,000. Interest rate is two points below to two points above Prime.

Child Care Micro-loan Fund
www.community-minded.org
25 W. Main St. Suite 310, Spokane, WA 99201
509-209-2613
Loans up to $5000 to licensed family child care homes and $25,000 to centers for start-up facility costs, health and safety improvements, minor renovations of licensed child care businesses, and operational equipment acquisition. 30 hours of free technical assistance and training. **Counties served: Ferry, Lincoln, Pend Oreille, Spokane, Stevens**

Childcare Microloans (CCML)
www.bfcog.us
509-943-9185, kfast@bfcog.us
Financing for childcare providers to become or continue to be licensed. Loans range from $500 to $5,000 for family home childcare providers, and up to $25,000 for child care centers. Eligible uses include safety items, equipment, fencing, etc. **Counties: Adams, Asotin, Benton, Chelan, Clark, Columbia, Douglas, Franklin, Garfield, Grant, Kittitas, Klickitat, Okanogan, Skamania, Walla Walla, Whitman, and Yakima.**

Clearwater Economic Development Association (CEDA)
www.clearwater-eda.org
1626 6th Ave., Lewiston, ID 83501
208-746-0015
Loans from $2,500 to $150,000 in **Clearwater, Idaho, Latah, Lewis** and **Nez Perce** Co in Idaho where conventional financing is not available. Technical assistance provided to borrowers.

Coastal Revolving Loan Fund
www.kitsapeda.org
Kitsap Economic Development Alliance
4312 Kitsap Way, Suite 103
Bremerton, WA 98312
360-479-3712
Low interest loans for start-up projects, expansion or purchase to create jobs in areas affected by fishing and timber industry declines. Max $50,000 **Counties served: Clallam, Jefferson, Grays Harbor, Pacific or Wahkiakum**

Community Capital Development (CCD)
http://seattleccd.com/drupal
1437 South Jackson, Seattle, WA 98144
206-324-4330
See listing on page 17.

CREDiT Rural Development Loans
www.bfcog.us/econ.html
509-943-9185, atackett@bfcog.us
Funds the amount between conventional financing available and the amount needed, of up to 75% of total project costs ($10,000 to $250,000) for start-ups or existing private for-profit and non-profit businesses of **Benton, Franklin, Walla Walla and Columbia** counties involved in manufacturing, value-added processing, service and retail operations. Interest rate: 2 pts below to 2 pts above Prime.

Microloan Revolving Fund (MRF)
www.bfcog.us
509-943-9185, kfast@bfcog.us
Provides financing to for-profit, independently owned and operated start-ups or expanding businesses that are unable to secure conventional financing. Range from $500 to $35,000. Funds can be used for equipment, machinery, inventory, operating capital, fixtures, and furniture. Interest rates vary. Maximum loan term is six years. **Serves Benton, Franklin, Columbia, Garfield, Asotin, Whitman, and Spokane counties.**

Panhandle Area Council
www.pacni.org
208-772-0584; paulferg@pacni.org
Offers SBA MicroLoan Program in **Boundary, Bonner, Kootenai, Shoshone, and Benewah** counties in Idaho.

Rural Community Development Resources (RCDR) - rcdr.biz
24 S. 3rd Ave, Yakima, WA 98902
509-453-5133; rcdr@charter.net
Provides business assistance, training, and microloan programs from $2,000 to $50,000 in the greater **Yakima** area for equipment, inventory, working capital, franchise purchases and/or cash flow restructuring.

SNAP Financial Access
www.snapwa.org
212 S. Wall St, Spokane, WA 99201
509-456-7174, ext 111;
Heyamoto@snapwa.org
New SBA microloan lender. Provides training, counseling and microloans from $500-$50,000 to low-to-moderate income entrepreneurs in **Spokane County.** Matches fund for entrepreneurs saving for projective business thru Individual Development Accounts. Has Access Green Loans to create jobs and promote "green" or sustainable business practices. SNAP's Business Resource Center is an entrepreneurial l brary available to the public by appointment.

SNEDA
www.sneda.org
715 E. Sprague Ave., Spokane, WA 99202
509-444-7633
For **Spokane** and surrounding areas, SNEDA, offers technical assistance in the form of business and counseling and loans loans of $5,000—$100,000. Can be a source of loan gap funding too.

Tri-County Economic Development District (TEDD)
www.teddonline.com
986 South Main, Ste A, Colville, WA 99114
509-684-4571 or 800-776-7318
Provides rural and revolving loan funds that can go up to $250,000, as well as Microloans in **Adams, Asotin, Ferry, Garfield, Grant, Lincoln, Pend Oreille, Stevens, Whitman, and rural Spokane County.**

WA Assistive Technology Foundation
http://www.washingtonaccessfund.org/
100 S. King Street, Suite 280
Seattle, Washington 98104
206-328-5116; info@watf.org
TTY: 1-800-214-8731
Nonprofit lender offers access loans for assistive technology, home and vehicle accessibility mods. Microloans ranging from $250 to $1,000.

Washington CASH
www.washingtoncash.org
2100 24th Ave S, Suite 380
Seattle, WA 98144
206-352-1945, info@washingtoncash.org
Helps people with low-incomes start and grow businesses. Services include: 20 hours of business training, loans begin at $500 and increase to $5,000. Ongoing technical assistance and peer support. SBA microloans from $500 to $50,000.

"Persistence is important. Develop a supportive banking relationship. Be adamant about record keeping to support capital access. Give your lender confidence in you and your product."

Richard Clemson, Pasta USA, Spokane, WA
SBA 504 loan recipient

VENTURE CAPITAL

Small Business Investment Company (SBIC)
www.sba.gov/inv
SBICs are privately owned and managed investment funds, licensed and regulated by SBA, that use their own capital - plus funds borrowed with an SBA guarantee - to make equity and debt investments in qualifying small businesses. The SBA does not invest directly into small business through SBICs. SBIC financing is not appropriate for all types of businesses and financing needs, but is one of many SBA programs designed to suit the varied needs of America's small businesses.

Bancshares Capital, L.P.
16118 72nd Ave W., Edmonds, WA 98026
(206)948-1195, bancshares_lp@msn.com
Investment policy: Early-stages high tech.
Investment type: E-commerce, software, digital media, telecom, and healthcare.

Fluke Venture Partners
www.flukeventures.com
11400 SE 6th Street, Suite 230
Bellevue, WA 98004
425-453-4590, gabelein@flukeventures.com
Preferred initial investment size: $1,000,000 - $2.5 to $4 million
Investment policy: Seed to second stage.
Investment type: Technology, healthcare and consumer-oriented companies.
Geographic preference: U.S. Pacific NW

NW Entrepreneur Network
http://www.nwen.org/
711 6th Avenue N.
Seattle, WA 98109
206-420-0226; info@nwen.org
Helps entrepreneurs make connections and access the resources they need to succeed. Focuses on helping entrepreneurs build their business network. They provide the knowledge, mentoring, and access to investors that creates and grows successful companies.

Free SBA Loan Briefings

SBA-backed loans are made by participating lenders and are used to fund start-up and existing service, retail construction, manufacturing businesses, and more.

Attend a loan briefing to find out:
- types of loans available, eligibility and credit requirements
- things you need to prepare for a lender
- lenders who have been actively doing small business loans
- SBA resources to help you get ready

Loan Briefing Locations
www.sba.gov/wa for dates and times

Seattle
Noon to 1:00 pm
2nd & 4th Thursday of each month
SBA Education & Training Center
2401 Fourth Ave, Suite 450
E-mail: workshops@sba.gov

Spokane
Noon to 1:00 pm
1st & 3rd Thursday of each month
SBA Training Room
801 W. Riverside Ave. Suite 444
509-353-2800

Offered quarterly in:

Federal Way - Noon to 1:30 pm
E-mail: Cosette@federalwaychamber.com

Olympia - 1:00 pm – 2:30 pm
E-mail: info@thurstonchamber.com

Tacoma - 11:00 am - 12:30 pm
www.tacomachamber.org
click on calendar/upcoming events

Unable to attend a loan briefing in person? Go virtual.
Noon to 1 p.m. - Every Thursday each month
Participate via ReadyTalk. As a virtual attendee, use your phone to hear the presenter and view the Microsoft Power Point presentation on your computer.

On the phone: **1-866-740-1260**   Access Code: **3109402**
On the computer: **www.readytalk.com** Access Code: **3109402**

Credit Reports – Where to Get Yours

In accordance with the Fair and Accurate Credit Transactions Act (FACT Act), you have the right to obtain one free copy of your credit report a year from each of the three major credit reporting agencies.

www.annualcreditreport.com provides consumers with a centralized and secure means to request and obtain their free credit reports once every 12 months. This site provides credit reports but does not provide credit scores, or more specifically FICO® scores. **Go online to www.myfico.com/**

Review your personal credit report from each credit reporting agency. Make sure to notify your lender of any incorrect information present in your credit report. You can dispute any errors by contacting the credit reporting agencies directly.

Business owners and entrepreneurs should check their business credit reports for accuracy before submitting loan or credit applications. To get copies of your business credit report, contact one of the business credit reporting agencies such as Dun & Bradstreet online at **www.dnb.com**.

Equifax	**Experian**	**TransUnion**
800-685-1111	888-397-3742	800-888-4213
www.equifax.com	**www.experian.com**	**www.transunion.com**

SBA Small Business Size Standards
www.sba.gov/size

SBA regulations define what is considered a "small" business concern for purposes of obtaining financial, managerial and government contract procurement assistance. Under the size criteria, one set of standards for each industry applies to all SBA financial and government contract procurement programs.

Each North American Industry Classification System (NAICS) Code has a specific industry size standard. For complete rules, see Code of Federal Regulations, Chapter 13 Part 121. Available at the Government Bookstore, Jackson Federal Building, 915 2nd Avenue, Seattle, or at the Seattle Public Library

Questions about specific industries not listed? Call 206-553-8546 or e-mail sizestandards@sba.gov

AGRICULTURE: Crops and livestock (except beef cattle feedlots and chicken egg farms) - 3 fiscal year average annual receipts do not exceed $750,000.

Beef Cattle Feedlots	$ 2,000,000
Chicken Egg Farms	$12,500,000
Ornamental Nursery Products	$ 750,000
Animal Aquaculture & Animal Specialty Farms	$ 750,000
Agricultural Services-Planting, Harvesting, etc.	$ 7,000,000
Fishing, Hunting, & Trapping	$ 4,000,000

CONSTRUCTION: General construction size standard is $33.5 million average annual receipts for the past three fiscal years. Size standard for special trade contractors is $14.0 million average annual receipts for the past three fiscal years.

TRANSPORTATION: Considered small if average annual receipts for the past 3 fiscal years do not exceed the specified amount:

Passenger Transport - Bus Service	$ 7,000,000
Trucking	$25,500,000
Storage/Warehousing	$25,500,000
Travel Agencies	$ 3,500,000
Freight Forwarding	$ 7,000,000
Tour Operators	$ 7,000,000
Water Transportation - freight or passenger	500 Employees
Air Transportation/Air Courier	1,500 Employees

MANUFACTURING: A business primarily engaged in manufacturing is considered small if its average number of employees does not exceed 500 over the preceding completed 12 calendar months (with some exceptions up to 1,500 employees).

SERVICE: A concern primarily engaged in a service industry is considered small if its average annual receipts do not exceed $7,000,000 for the past three fiscal years.
Sample Exceptions

Dry Cleaning Plants	$ 4,500,000
Power Laundry/Linen Supply	$14,000,000
Car/Truck Rental	$25,500,000
Detectives, and Armored Car Service	$12,500,000
Engineering Services	$ 4,500,000
Building Cleaning & Maintenance	$16,500,000
Computer Programming /Software/Data Processing	$25,000,000
Accounting, Auditing, Bookkeeping	$ 8,500,000

RETAIL: In most industry classifications, a retail concern is considered a small business if its average annual receipts do not exceed $7,000,000 for the past 3 fiscal years (500 employees for government procurement of supplies).

Sample Exceptions	
Mobile Home Dealers	$13,000,000
Department Stores	$27,000,000
Variety Stores	$11,000,000
Grocery Stores	$27,000,000
Gasoline Service Stations	$ 9,000,000
Motor Vehicle Dealers (New)	$29,000,000
Motor Vehicle Dealers (Used)	$23,000,000
Most Clothing Stores	$ 9,000,000
Household Appliance Stores	$ 9,000,000
Radio & TV Stores	$ 9,000,000
Heating Oil Dealers	50 employees

WHOLESALE: A concern primarily engaged in wholesaling is considered small if its average number of employees does not exceed 100 over the preceding completed 12 calendar months (500 employees for government procurement of supplies).

"Contractors are gun shy about doing work with the government because of the paperwork. But if you're capable and have the experience, the door can be opened - despite not being large. There are so many federal agencies; it's like a contractor's dream."

Randy Smith, Northcon Inc., Hayden Idaho
HUBZone, SDB Certified, and former 8(a)

Government Contracting: Where do I start?

Use this checklist to help you prepare to bid on private and government procurement opportunities.

☐ Get a computer and get on the Internet! Even if you don't have your own website, you must at least have an e-mail address to conduct business with the government

☐ Find your DUNS (Data Universal Numbering System) number. Get this number by calling Dun & Bradstreet at 866-705-5711 or visit their website at **http://fedgov.dnb.com/webform/displayHomePage.do**. This free of charge process only takes a few minutes.

☐ Find your NAIC North American Industry Classification System codes. The code(s)s describes what your business does.

Go to **http://www.census.gov/eos/www/naics/** to determine your NAICS code. Be sure to keep these codes handy, as you may need them when filling out government registrations or searching for bids.

☐ Register your business with the Central Contracts Registration. Their website is **www.bpn.gov/ccr** Companies who want to do business with the Federal Government are required to be registered in CCR.

☐ After signing up for CCR, be sure to complete your ORCA (Online Representations and Certification application) at **https://orca.bpn.gov**. This registration allows you to enter your reps and certs information just once for use on all future government contracts.

☐ After signing up for CCR, be sure to fill out the additional information to register in the Dynamic Small Business Search at the CCR website. This website provides a database for government contractors and prime contractors to use when they are looking for vendors. **http://dsbs.sba.gov/dsbs/search/dsp_dsbs.cfm**

☐ Be sure to keep track of your CAGE code. If you don't have a CAGE code, you will get one when you sign up for the Central Contractor's Registration. The Federal Government may use this code when pays you for goods and services.

☐ Find your local PTAC by visiting the website at **www.washingtonptac.org**. They assist with registrations, answers questions and offers workshops. See page 22

☐ Minority and women-owned business should apply for certification through the WA State Office of Minority and Women's Business Enterprise at **www.omwbe.wa.gov.**

OMWBE certification helps you get contracts with state and local agencies and schools. There special loan program has discounted interest rates.

☐ Your company may qualify for SBA procurement certifications such as HubZone or 8(a). Go on-line to **http://training.sba.gov:8000/assessment** to access the **8(a) Business Development assessment tool.** This customized tool takes about 10 minutes to complete and helps small business owners determine their eligibility. Also see page 23.

☐ Most Federal agencies have government contracting specialists. Go to **http://www.osdbu.gov/offices.html** to find agency reps who work with small businesses.

☐ Visit the Fed Biz Opps website at **https://www.fbo.gov** You can also register as a vendor and have bids e-mailed to you.

☐ Visit General Services Administration at **www.gsa.gov** Check out the GSA schedule and see the variety of goods and services listed. Consider applying for a GSA contract (called a "schedule") which allows government buyers to purchase from you at a prearranged price.

☐ Don't forget about your local government agencies and entities. Check with your local cities, ports, school districts, counties and other local agencies for information on their purchasing practices, small works rosters, vendors' lists, etc.

Tips to Remember

- Print out online applications and fill them out on paper before doing them online.

- Always keep copies of application you have done online and/or mailed and faxed in. And, be sure you write down the dates you submitted the applications on the copies.

- Always write down and keep any passwords, registration numbers, MPINS or TPINS. These can be very hard to replace if you lose them!

- Don't hesitate to call the help lines on websites if you have questions. Once again, keep track of who and when you called.

- If you call a help line and aren't satisfied with the person you are talking to, document the call, hang up, call back and talk to someone else.

Keep documentation of everything! You may need it in the future.

Procurement Technical Assistance Centers PTAC

PTAC is designed to assist businesses with any aspect of federal, state and local government contracting. The PTAC provides assistance with:

Computerized Bid Match Service
They search numerous government databases for bid leads that match your company. $100 annual fee for this optional service. All other services are free.

Interpretation of Solicitations
Help decipher solicitations by reviewing contract clauses, terms, definitions and requirements.

Assistance with government registrations and certifications
CCR (Central Contractor Registration), CAGE (Commercial and Gov't Entity) codes DUNS (Data Universal Numbering System) (SDB) Small Disadvantaged Business, 8(a) certification, and HUBZone (Historically Underutilized Business Zone)

Training and Seminars
Marketing Assistance
Specifications, Standards and Drawing
Assistance in locating necessary documents for solicitations.

PTAC Locations

PTAC Serving Washington State
www.washingtonptac.org
Located with Snohomish County EDC
728 134th St. SW, Suite 128
Everett, WA 98204
Kylene Binder, Program Manager
425-248-4215; kbinder@snoedc.org
Serving Counties: Chelan, Douglas, Grant, Island, Kittitas, Klickitat, Okanogan, San Juan, Skagit, Snohomish, Whatcom & Yakima

Outreach Centers

Eastern Washington PTAC
www.gsiptac.org
www.facebook.com/wa-ptac
Operated by Greater Spokane Incorporated
801 Riverside Avenue, Spokane, WA 99201
Leslie Miller, 509-321-3641
ptac@greaterspokane.org
Serving Counties: Adams, Asotin, Columbia, Ferry, Garfield, Lincoln, Pend Oreille, Stevens, Spokane, Walla Walla, Whitman

Highline Community College
23835 Pacific Hwy S. - Bldg MS 99-101
Kent, WA 98032
Darrell Sundell, 206-878-3710 x 5146
dsundell@highline.edu
Serving King and Pierce counties

Idaho Dept of Commerce & PTAC
www.commerce.idaho.gov
700 West State, Boise, ID 83720-0093
Gary Moore, 1-800-842-5858; 208-334-2470
gary.moore@commerce.idaho.gov
Information about contracting opportunities.

Kitsap Economic Development Alliance
4312 Kitsap Way, Suite 103
Bremerton, WA 98312
Becky Newton, 877-465-4872
newton@kitsapeda.org
Serving Counties: Clallam, Grays Harbor, Jefferson, Kitsap, Mason, Pacific, Wahkiakum

Native American PTAC
www.nativeptac.org
650 South Orcas St, Suite 219
Seattle, WA 98108
206-816-6596; information@nativeptac.org
Serves AK, WA, OR, ID and Western MT

Thurston County EDC
665 Woodland Sq. Lp. SE #201
Lacey, WA 98503
Tiffany Scroggs, 360-754-6320
tscroggs@thurstonedc.com
Serving Counties: Clark, Cowlitz, Lewis, Skamania, Thurston

PTAC at Tri-City Regional Chamber of Commerce
7130 W. Grandridge Blvd, Suite C
Kennewick, WA 99336
Ashley Bennington-Coronado, 509-736-0510
ashley.coronado@tricityregionalchamber.com
Serving counties: Benton, Franklin

Gov't Contracting Resources

Business Links
WSU Tri-Cities
2710 University Drive
Richland, WA 99352-1671
509-372-7142; links@tricity.wsu.edu

Commerce Business Daily
http://www.cbd-net.com/

Dun & Bradstreet (D&B)
www.dnb.com
Provides information on businesses and corporations for use in credit decisions, B2B marketing and supply chain management.

Federal Business Opportunity
www.fedbizopps.gov

Federal Acquisition Regulations (FARs)
http://farsite.hill.af.mil
A single source repository of Federal Acquisition Regulations for all the military services, this site serves as an easy-to-use research tool providing links to most of the various FARs, supplements and updates.

General Services Administration (GSA)
www.gsa.gov
GSA contractors list products in the GSA catalog for sales to government.

GSA Federal Supply Service
www.fss.gsa.gov
Qualified businesses may obtain a GSA Federal Supply Schedule contract and post their products and services on the GSA Advantage website where federal buyers can procure the products and services to satisfy all their business needs.

Government Web Portal
www.usa.gov
FirstGov supplies direct online access to official federal, state, local and tr bal government transactions, services and information.

North American Industry Classificaiton System NAICS
http://www.census.gov/eos/www/naics/
NAICS is the standard used to classify business establishments for the purpose of collecting, analyzing, and publishing statistical data related to the U.S. business economy.

Small Disadvantaged Business Certification SDB
https://orca.bpn.gov
SDB is no longer certified through SBA. It is a self certify designation.

Small Business Innovation Research (SBIR)
www.acq.osd.mil/sadbu/sbir
Learn how to obtain funding for relevant, early stage R&D projects in small technology companies through this program offered by the Department of Defense.

Washington State Department of General Administration
www.ga.wa.gov
360-902-0990
Encourages state contracts for small firms.

WA State Office of Minority and Women's Business Enterprises (OMWBE)
www.omwbe.wa.gov
Olympia 360-753-9693
Tacoma 253-680-7770
Increases the participation of bona fide minority and women's businesses in state public works contracting and purchasing of goods and services. Provides certification of qualifying small businesses, conducts compliance reviews and monitors the use of certified firms by state agencies.

www.womenbiz.gov
Gateway for women-owned businesses selling to the government

SBA Government Contracting Certification Programs - www.sba.gov/contracting

8(a) Program

The program helps small disadvantaged businesses compete in the market place, gain access to federal and private procurement markets, and prepare small disadvantaged firms for procurement and other business opportunites. The focus is to provide business development support, such as mentoring, procurement assistance, business counseling, training, financial assistance, surety bonding and other management and technical assistance.

Available to businesses that:
- meet SBA's small business size standards
- have been operating for at least two years prior to application
- are owned by persons who are U.S. citizens
- are owned at least 51% by one or more socially and economically disadvantaged individuals

Socially disadvantaged groups include:

- Black American
- Hispanic American
- Native American
- Asian Pacific American
- Subcontinent Asian American

Others must provide evidence as to how they have been discriminated

Economically disadvantaged businesses must have:
- personal net worth must be less than $250,000 (equity in primary residence and in business excluded)
- a product or service regularly purchased by the federal government

Apply online at **www.sba.gov/8abd** go to **"Applying to the 8a Program"**

For more information about the SBA 8a Program contact:
Western Washington	206-553-7341; diana.drake@sba.gov
Eastern WA & North ID	509-353-2810; sharon.pataky@sba.gov
Idaho	208-334-9004, ext 349; irene.gonzalez@sba.gov

HUBZone - Historically Underutilized Business Zone

Provides "place-based" opportunities for federal prime contract and subcontract benefits.

Available to small businesses:
that meet SBA Small Business size standards
- principal office is located in a HUBZone which includes Indian Country lands and military bases closed by BRAC;
- at least 51% owned and controlled by persons who are U.S. citizens, or CDC, an agricultural cooperative, or an indian tr be; and
- at least 35% of its employees must be HUBZone residents.

Apply online: **www.sba.gov/hubzone**
Questions? **hubzone@sba.gov** or **202-205-8885**

Women-Owned Small Business Federal Contract Program WOSB
www.sba.gov/wosb
To qualify for contract set asides, register in CCR and self certify as a WOSB or EDWOSB (Economically Disadvantaged) in ORCA, plus upload extra documentation.
Contact: **wosb@sba.gov** or **1-800-827-5722**

SBA Procurement Center Representative PCR
PCRs increase the small business share of Federal procurement awards by initiating small business set-asides, reserving procurements for competition among small business firms; providing small business sources to Federal buying activities; and counseling small firms. In addition, PCRs, advocate for the breakout of items for full and open competition to affect savings to the Federal Government.
Contact: **kevin.michael@sba.gov** or call **253-931-7161**

Size Standards - more information on page 20

**Central Contract Registration
(Dynamic Small Business Search)
www.bpn.gov/ccr
866-606-8220 - 8 am to 8 pm EST**

CCR registration is a MUST for any small business wishing to do business with the federal government.

❑ Available free of charge to small firms seeking federal, state or private- sector contracts

❑ Provides opportunity to create, view and update business profile

❑ Links firms to current procurement opportunities through electronic connection

❑ Creates a marketing tool to sell your product or service to both government and private sector

❑ Provides access to buyers looking for qualified vendors

Tip - after completing CCR registration:

1. Make sure to register or update your SBA Profile.
2. Designate your primary NAICS code.

**FREE Government Contract Briefing
4th Thursday of each month
8:30 am - 9:30 am**

SBA Education & Training Center
2401 Fourth Ave, Suite 450
Seattle, WA 98121

Interested in gaining access to federal, state and local procurement markets?

This briefing:

- Prepares small firms for government contracts and other procurement opportunities

- Provides information on federal government certification

- Covers resources available to assist with selling to the government.

Register by e-mail
workshops@sba.gov

Surety Bond Guarantee Program SBG

http://www.sba.gov/content/bond-agencies-state

The Surety Bond Guarantee Program helps small and emerging contractors obtain bid, performance and payment bonds. The SBA guarantees up to 90% of a bond issued by a surety company for construction, service, supply and manufacturing contracts. To qualify as a small business an applicant's annual receipts must meet the NAICS standard.

Seattle Bond Office handles applications for bond guarantees on behalf of contractors domiciled in nine western states and thirteen southern states.
Call 206-553-2746 for more information.

Washington State Bond Agencies

Western Washington

Contractors Bonding & Insurance Company Inc. (CBIC)
1213 Valley Street
Seattle, WA 98109-0271
Brian Schick, brians@cbic.com; Mark Noma, markn@cbic.com
Mark Harbak, markhk@cbic.com 1-800-765-2242; 206-628-7200

Construction Bonding & Management Services of WA, Inc.
11050 5th Ave. N.E., Suite # 206
Seattle, WA 98125
Nicholas Fix, Rick Fix
1-800-742-8815; 206-361-9693

Hartford Fire Insurance Company
Larry Christianson
520 Pike Tower, Suite #1004
Seattle, WA 98101
206-346-0121

Integrity Surety LLC
www.integritysurety.com
938 N 200th Street, Suite D
Seattle, WA 98133
Kara Skinner, 206-546-1397;

McDonald Insurance Group
Jeff Stewart
Kirkland, WA 98083
425-897-5974; jeff@mcdonaldins.com

Superior Underwriters
2027 152nd Avenue N.E., C-24
Redmond, WA 98052
Johanis Sinon, Margaret Robbins
425-643-5200; mardier@gsusuperior.com

WUIA dba The Bond Shop
3425 Broadway
Everett, WA 98206
Mary Fauré, 1-800-726-8771, Ext. 3561, 425-317-3561
maryf@thebondshop.net

Eastern Washington

Contractors Bonding & Insurance Company, Inc. (CBIC)
N. 901 Monroe, Suite # 340
Spokane, WA 99201
Marci Houts, Hans Rauth, hansr@cbic.com
1-800-368-2242; 509-326-2244

Payne Financial Group Inc
Jim Majeskey
Spokane, WA 99220
1-800-736-5592; 509-455-6767

Contracting Opportunities for Service-Disabled Veterans

Small Business Concerns owned and controlled by service-disabled veterans has been established under The Veterans Benefits Act of 2003 - Public Law 108-183. This act assists federal agencies in meeting the 3% veteran contracting goal.

Federal contracting officers may now set-aside or award sole-source contracts to Service-Disabled Veteran Owned (SDVO) Small Business Concerns (SBC).

Eligibility:

1. 51% or more of the SDVO SBC is owned by one or more service-disabled veterans.

2. Management and daily business operations is controlled by one or more service-disabled veterans or the spouse of such veteran if the veteran is permanently and severely disabled.

3. At the time of contract offer, an SDVO SBC is small as defined by the size standard corresponding to the NAICS code (13 CFR 121.201) assigned to the contract.

Small business concerns **self-certify.** You should obtain a letter from the VA certifying that you are a service-disabled veteran in the event another business protests your award.

Contract Opportunities - Department of Veterans Affairs
www.vip.vetbiz.gov
Register with the VA and submit additional documentation. As a registered Veteran-Owned and Service-Disabled businesses you will receive:

1. Priority contracting opportunities under VA's Veterans First Buying Authority.
2. Special consideration from prime contractors and federal government agencies.
3. Notices of contracting opportunities.

Contact for U.S. Dept of VA/The Center for Veterans Enterprise
vip@mail.va.gov or **866-584-2344 or 202-303-3260**

Regional contacts for Veterans

VBOC Veterans Business Outreach Center
seattleccd.com/drupal/VBOC
1437 S. Jackson Street, Seattle WA 98144
Lynn Trepp, 206-324-4330 ext 139
info@seattleccd.com

Seattle SBA Veteran Representative
patricia.jordan@sba.gov

Resources for Veterans

VBOC
Veterans Business Outreach Center
seattleccd.com/drupal/VBOC
1437 S. Jackson Street, Seattle WA 98144
Lynn Trepp, 206-324-4330 ext 139
info@seattleccd.com
SBA Region 10's VBOC operated by
Community Capital Development in Seattle.
Assists veterans, service-disabled veterans,
reservists, National Guard members, and
active-duty service members preparing to
transition from military service to business
ownership. Delivers business counseling,
training, and coordinates resources so
veteran entrepreneurs can:
- Create a competitive business plans
- Prepare loan request packages
- Obtain financing
- Manage a business profitably
- Expand their business networks
**Serves Washington, Oregon, Alaska,
and Idaho.**

WDVA Veterans Linked Deposit Program
www.dva.wa.gov/linked%20deposit.html
800-562-0132 Option 1
communications@dva.wa.gov
For certified Veteran-owned businesses in
WA. Decreases interest rates up to 2% on
small business loans. Loan limit $1 million
per loan, 10 year maximum term. See
participating bank list online. Commercial
financing for lines of credit, accounts
receivables, working capital, equipment
purchases, and real property acquisition.
Veteran business owners must register
through **www.vip.VetBiz.gov** and WA
Veteran/Servicemember Owned Registry
www.dva.wa.gov/BusinessRegistry.

VetFran
Veterans Transition Franchise Initiative
www.franchise.org/veteran-franchise.aspx
Nearly 400 member companies of the
International Franchise Association offer
financial incentives such as specific
discounts on franchise fees to honorably
discharged veterans interested in franchise
business ownership.

SBA Patriot Express Loans
www.sba.gov/patriotexpress
Seattle - mark.costello@sba.gov, 206-553-7312
Spokane - ted schinzel@sba.gov, 509-353-2806
Can be used for start-up, expansion,
equipment purchases, working capital,
inventory, and business-occupied real
estate purchases. Fast turn-around time
for loan approvals by participating lenders
nationwide. Contact local SBA office for list
of lenders who do Patriot Express loans.
Amount: Up to $500,000
Interest rate: 2.25 – 4.75 % over prime
Guaranty: 85% for loans up to $150,000
             75% for loans over $150,000

Resources for Minorities

AHANA Business & Professional Association
www.ahana.org/
25 W. Main, Suite 300
Spokane, WA 99201
509-209-2634; bcabildo@ahana.org
AHANA stands for Asian/Hispanic/
African/Native American. Support group
for entrepreneurs of color in the Inland
Northwest.

Black Dollar Days Task Force (BDDTF)
www.blackdollar.org
116 21st Avenue
Seattle, WA 98122
206-323-0534
A nonprofit organization that offers
entrepreneurial training, technical
assistance, and information and referral
services to existing business owners and
individuals interested in starting a business.
Small loans available through the BDDTF
Campaign 5000 Loan Fund.

CDCC - Contractor Development and Competitiveness Center
**http://www.urbanleague.org/index.php/
departments/cdcc**
105 - 14th Avenue, 1st Floor
Seattle, WA 98122 - 206-323-0721
Assistance and support to small businesses
who are not fully participating in the
contracting opportunities in this region.

Contractors Resource Center
2301 S. Jackson, Suite 1016
Seattle, WA 98144
206-329-7804
Provides a program accessible to minority
firms in the construction industry.

Dept of the Interior Loan Program
www.bia.gov
Office of Indian Energy and Economic Dev
Chandler Allen, 202-208-7166
LoanGuaranty@bia.gov
Loans up to $500,000 for individuals, up to
$5 million for Indian-owned businesses, and
up to $12 million for tribe or tribally owned
businesses. Projects must have a positive
economic impact to the tribal reservation or
service area. Borrowers must contribute a
20% equity injection. At least 51% federally
recognized ownership by American Indian,
tribe or Alaska Native is required.

Idaho Dept. of Transportation
www.itd.idaho.gov/civil/overview.htm
Bureau of Civil Rights
**Disadvantaged Business Enterprise
Support Services**
P.O. Box 7129, Boise, ID 83707-1129
208-334-4442
Program to assist minority, women
and disadvantaged business owners in
developing and promoting their businesses
in the highway construction industry.
Provides training, certification, and info.

Minority Business Development Center
http://www.mbecwa.com/
1437 S. Jackson Street, Suite 301
Seattle, WA 98144 - 206-267-3131
Assists minority businesses that earning
potential of $500,000 or more in revenues
or are capable of generating significant
employment and long-term economic
growth. Must be 51% owned and operated
by a recognized ethnic minority.

Native American PTAC
www.nativeptac.org/contactus.html
6520 South 190th Street – 2nd floor
Kent, WA 98032.

MBDC - www.mbecwa.com
Northwest Minority Enterprise Center
1437 S. Jackson Street, Suite 301
Seattle, WA 98144
206-267-3131
The mission is to create and develop
business opportunities for minority firms
between major private sector corporations
and public agencies fostering economic
development in the communities.z

NNDF - www.thenndf.org
Northwest Native Development Fund
PO Box 148, Nespelem, WA 99155
509-634-2624
Serves the **Colville, Spokane and
Kalispell Indian Reservations** as well as
tribal members, descendents, and those
employed by tribally owned businesses.
It works with local lenders and provides
financial and technical assistance for those
who may not qualify for outside funding
to help individuals build assets including
small business ownership. A counselor
aids individuals seeking to start or expand a
business through business plan, marketing
plan and financial plan development.
Provides home and employee loans.

ONABEN - Oregon Native American Business & Entrepreneurial Network
www.indianpreneurship.com
503-968-1500
ONABEN offers training and support
focused on developing entrepreneurship in
Native American communities throughout
the Inland NW.

RCDR - www.rcdr.biz/
Rural Community Dev Resources
Attn: Luz Gutierrez
24 S. 3rd Ave., Yakima, WA 98909
509-453-5133; RCDR@charter.net
Specializing in the start-up or expansion of
small businesses, RCDR provides business
assistance and training resources, as well
as an SBA microloan program in the greater
Yakima area.

SBA - 8(a) Program - see page 23

OMWBE - www.omwbe.wa.gov
**WA Office of Minority and Women's
Business Enterprise**
Olympia 360-753-9693
Tacoma 253-680-7770

Business Resources

International Trade

U.S. Commercial Service
U.S. Department of Commerce
U.S. Export Assistance Center
www.buyusa.gov/seattle
Cooperative effort of the Commercial Service of the U.S. Dept. of Commerce, the Export Finance Assistance Center of Washington and the SBA. Assists with accessing and developing an international marketing strategy, providing customized market research, international trade data, leads, and contacts for Trade promotion events, programs and publications. Info on export loans, loan guarantees and export credit insurance is available.

Seattle - 4th and Vine Building
Pru Balatero, 206-553-0051
pru.balatero@sba.gov

Spokane - Eastern Washington region
U.S. Department of Commerce
www.buyusa.gov/spokane
801 W. Riverside Avenue, Suite 100
Spokane, WA 99201
509-353-2625

Boise - Serves Idaho, including Panhandle area
U.S. Department of Commerce
www.buyusa.gov/Boise/
700 West State Street, 2nd Floor
Boise, ID 83720
208-364-7791; amy.benson@trade.gov

Bureau of Industry and Security
www.bis.doc.gov
408-998-7402
Processes licenses for US exports

Idaho Dept. of Commerce & Labor
Division of International Business
http://commerce.idaho.gov/international
700 West State Street
Boise, ID 83720-0093
Commerce 208-334-2650 ext 2109
Promotes expansion of international trade and investment and support of international tourism; export assistance to Idaho firms.

International Trade Alliance ITA
www.intrade.org
601 W. Main Avenue, Suite 315
Spokane, WA 99201
509-413-1470; info@intrade.org
For companies in WA assists in establishing export markets. Understand what it takes to be export ready.

NW Trade Adjustment Assistance Center
www.nwtaac.org 206-622-2730
Provide assistance to US manufacturers affected by import competition. Services include market studies, engineering surveys, cost reduction programs, product development, management information systems and financial services.

Port of Seattle
www.portseattle.org
206-728-3000 Seattle
509-742-9362 Spokane
Offers information on shipping goods internationally.

Trade Dev Alliance of Greater Seattle
www.seattletradealliance.com
Promote trade interests in domestic and international markets of Greater Seattle, King, Pierce, and Snohomish Counties.

U.S. Customs and Border Protection
www.customs.gov
206-553-6944 Seattle;
509-353-2833 Spokane
Assess and collect duties, taxes and fees on imported merchandise, enforce customs and related laws, and the administer certain navigational laws and treaties.

WA Small Business Development Center
Export Readiness Center
www.wsbdc.org/exporting
See page 13

Washington State Department of Agriculture
http://agr.wa.gov/Marketing/default.aspx
International Marketing and Export Assistance - 360-902-1915
Assists Washington companies to export food and agricultural products. Works closely with the U.S. Dept. of Agriculture to promote exports and the Governor's Office and industry to resolve foreign trade barriers.

World Trade Center Tacoma
www.wtcta.org
253-396-1022 or info@wtcta.org

Chambers of Commerce

Washington Chambers
www.wcce.org

Idaho Chambers
www.2chambers.com/idaho2.htm

Association of Washington Business
www.awb.org/index.asp

Independent Business Association
www.ibaw.net
16541 Redmond Way, Suite 336C
Redmond, WA 98052
425-453-8621
The voice of small business in Olympia. Lobbies on behalf of small business. Provides information on laws, regulations, and taxes.

National Federation of Independent Business (NFIB)
http://www.nfib.com/
4160 Sixth Avenue SE, Suite 201
Lacy, WA 98503
360-786-8675 or 1-800-NFIBNOW
NFIB's purpose is to influence Public Policy at the State and Federal level and be the resource for Small and Independent Business in America.

WA State Hispanic Chambers
www.awshcc.com
206-329-5534; info@awshcc.com

Economic Development Councils

Clearwater Economic Development Association (CEDA)
www.clearwater-eda.org
1626 6th Ave, Lewiston, ID 83501
208-746-0015
Operates in the public interest to improve economic opportunities, increase employment skills and sustain preferred lifestyles for residents, communities and businesses in North Central Idaho.

Jobs Plus
http://www.jobsplusonline.org/
202 Sherman Avenue
Coeur d'Alene, ID 83816
208-667-4753; Toll-Free 800-621-5600
North Idaho business recruiting. Provides information to businesses considering relocation and/or expansion to North Idaho.

Tri-County Industrial Development Council (TRIDEC) - www.tridec.org
Kennewick 509-735-1000
Serves Benton and Franklin counties. Assists companies interested in expanding to the Tri-Cities as well as resources for new and growing businesses located in the region.

WA Economic Development Councils
www.ecodevdirectory.com/washington.htm
EDCs across the state provide local business assistance resources, community profiles, seminars, industrial site information, export assistance, and financing assistance.

Technology Resources

Connect Northwest (WA, ID, and MT)
www.connectnw.org
509-358-2110; info@connectnw.org
Connects science and technology based companies with resources necessary to succeed. Provides coaching, mentoring, business plan and presentation preparation, seminars, and networking events.

Innovate Washington (New state agency)
Formed by merging Sirti and the Washington Technology Center –will assist innovative companies statewide with their technology commercialization needs. Its sector-based approach will bolster technology enterprises, starting with clean energy, while providing a range of support to young, innovative technology companies in others industries.

Sirti - www.sirti.org
665 N. Riverpoint Blvd
Spokane, WA 99202-1665
509-358-2000

Washington Technology Center (WTC)
www.watechcenter.org
300 Fluke Hall, Box 352140
Seattle, WA 98195-2140
206-685-1920; info@watechcenter.org

MIT Enterprise Forum of the Northwest
www.mitwa.org
206-283-9595 or www.iba@isomedia.com
Provides creative programs that educate
and foster innovative technology
companies.

Northwest Entrepreneur Network
www.nwen.org
425-564-5701
Helps entrepreneurs build their business
network. Provides the knowledge,
mentoring, and access to investors that
creates and grows successful companies.

**SBIR—Small Business Innovative
Research** - www.sba.gov/sbir
Funds early-stage R&D projects at small
technology companies that have the
potential for commercialization in the
private sector and/or military markets.

**For answers to technical questions
about specific SBIR solicitation**
www.dodsbir.net/sitis
sbirhelp@brtrc.com
Submit written question through the SBIR/
STTR Interactive Topic Information System
(SITIS). All questions and answers are
posted electronically for general viewing
until the solicitation closes.

Technology Alliance
www.technology-alliance.com
Statewide consortium of leaders from tech-
based businesses, research institutions,
and high tech trade associations. Focuses
are education, promoting WA as a tech
leader and fostering innovation. Alliance
of Angels program facilitates access to
capital.

Terabyte Triangle
www.terabytetriangle.com
In Spokane. Hosts Internet speeds up to
20 gigabits with "plug-and-go" locations for
startups and existing companies. A heavily
wired and wireless metro area ideal for
e-commerce, software development, and
multi-media businesses. TT also has state-
of-the-art wet labs ideal for bio-tech.

Tincan
www.tincan.org
509-744-0972; tincaninfo@tincan.org
Supports social, economic and community
development through the use of computer
technology and interactive media. Projects
include e-commerce curriculum development for secondary schools, a Young
Entrepreneurs Center for school and youth
groups, community technology centers.

**U.S. Dept of Energy
Energy Efficiency and Renewable
Energy**
http://www1.eere.energy.gov/industry
Contact point for inventors who are inter-
ested in participating in the U.S. Dept. of
Energy's Inventions and Innovation Program.

**Washington State Innovation
Assessment Center (IAC)**
http://www.business.wsu.edu/organizations/iac/
Washington State University
Pullman, WA 99164-4850
509-335-8842; jthornley@wsu.edu
Offers the Innovation Assessment Report
- which serves as an objective, comprehensive evaluation of your new product idea, a
patent search to determine if patents have
been issued for similar products.

**Washington Manufacturing Services
(WMS)** - www.wamfg.org
1-800-637-4634; info@wafmg.org
Help manufacturers become more
competitive in global markets.
Representatives help local manufacturers
develop an appropriate action plan to attain
cost savings and increased productivity.

More Resources

Attorney General - Washington Office
www.atg.wa.gov/Default.aspx
800-551-4636
Upholds the Consumer Protection Act and
enforces laws against anti-competitive
business practices. **In Idaho: 208-334-2424**

Better Business Bureau
www.thebbb.org - **Western Washington**
206-431-2222; info@thebbb.org
http://spokane.bbb.org/ - Spokane
800-356-1007; info@spokane.bbb.org
Maintains fair and honest business dealings
between consumers and businesses.

Business Waste Line
http://www.lhwmp.org/home/default.aspx
Hazardous Waste Management Program
Seattle 206-263-8899
Open Monday-Friday, 9 am - 12, 1 - 4 pm
Free hotline with quick answers to many
hazardous waste questions.

Commercial Kitchen Rental
www.kitchenrental.org
120 E. Wellesley, Spokane, WA 99207
509-868-5774
Fully equipped commercial kitchen.
Available 24/7 to help entrepreneurs build
small businesses with lowered risk and
minimized start-up costs.

Enterprise for Equity (E4E)
www.enterpriseforequity.org
360-704-3375
Entrepreneur training, peer support learning circles, and micro-credit assistance to
enterprising individuals with limited incomes
in the South Puget Sound area who dream
of owning a business.

Environmental Coalition of South Seattle
www.ecoss.org
Al Van Schaik; al@ecoss.org
206-767-0432 Seattle
253-573-1128 Tacoma
Assists with environmental and economic
development issues. Free consultations.

Executive Service Corps of Washington
http://www.escwa.org/
Seattle 206-682-6704 or execdir@escwa.org
Mostly retired business executives,
managers and community volunteers
contribute their expertise to help nonprofit
and public organizations statewide.

**Resource Venture - Business and
Industry** - www.resourceventure.org
Seattle 206-389-7304
Free info, assistance and referrals to
help businesses improve environmental
performance. Focused on waste prevention
and recycling, water conservation,
stormwater pollution prevention, and
sustainable building.

**Seattle Public Library
Small Business Center** - www.spl.org
Central L brary
1000 Fourth Ave., Seattle, WA 98104
206-386-4645 *Business Department*
206-386-4636 *Quick Information*
Provides resource material on small
business, financing, and international trade.

Spokane SNAP's Business Library
www.snapwa.org/node/275
212 South Wall
509-456-7174 x111 heyamoto@snapwa.org
Entrepreneurial library in downtown
Spokane. Open to the public by appt **U.S.
Government On-line Bookstore**
http://bookstore.gpo.gov
Order publications (books, maps, serials,
videos, CD-ROMs, subscriptions) for sale.

**Washington Society of Certified Public
Accountants** - www.wscpa.org
425-644-4800 or 800-272-8273
Provides referral services for small businesses in need of accounting and financial
management assistance.

Labeling

Bar Code Basics
www.barcodehq.com/primer.html

Clothing Labels Guidance
http://www.cpsc.gov/

RFID - Radio Frequency Identification
www.rfid.org

U.S. Dept. of Agriculture
www.fsis.usda.gov 509-533-2490
Labeling requirements for food

UPC - Universal Product Codes
www.gs1us.org
UPC Bar Codes for Product Packaging
800-543-8137 or 513-435-3870

AgriBusiness Resources

USDA Business & Industry (B&I) Loans
http://www.rurdev.usda.gov/wa/
http://www.rurdev.usda.gov/id/
Designed to encourage commercial financing of rural businesses, create and save rural jobs, and improve the economic climate of rural communities. The B&I program is lender-driven. L ke SBA, USDA guarantees the loan rather than lending directly. A commercial lender requests the B&I guarantee makes (and services) the loan. Lenders use their own forms, loan documents, and security instruments.

USDA B&I guarantees for rural business loans:
80% (maximum) guarantee cumulatively up to $5 million
70% (maximum) guarantee cumulatively from $5-10 million

USDA B&I Loan Sizes:
No minimum; up to $10 million and in some cases, $25 million. Usually B&I loans range from $200,000 to $5 million.

Rate: Lender's customary commercial interest rate
Fixed or variable

Term: Working capital – 7 years maximum
Equipment – 15 years maximum
Real estate – 30 years maximum

Structure: Balloons are not permitted. Reduced payments may be scheduled in the first 3 years.

Fees: Lender's reasonable and customary fees. USDA charges an initial guarantee fee equal to 2% of the guaranteed amt plus an annual renewal fee.

Authorized Loan Purposes: Real estate, buildings, leasehold improvements, equipment, inventory, & permanent working capital, professional services, feasibility study costs, loan fees & costs (including B&I guarantee fee). Lines of credit cannot be guaranteed.

Debt refinancing: The refinancing must create new jobs or secure existing jobs (e.g., by improving cash flow). If a lender wishes to refinance a loan already in their portfolio, this must be a secondary purpose (less than 50% of loan) & the loan must have been current for at least 12 months.

Commercial lease projects (retail centers, office buildings, industrial facilities, etc.):
No owner-occupancy required.
Must have enough committed tenants to break even.
New developments and renovation projects are eligible.
Transfer of ownership and debt refinancing are normally not eligible.

Community facility projects may be guaranteed if the financing is not tax-exempt.

Borrower Eligibility: Most types of enterprises qualify– manufacturing, wholesale, retail, service new or existing. Project must be in a rural area – beyond any 50,000+ population city and its urbanized periphery.

Ineligible businesses:
Owner-occupied and rental housing projects (Housing site development may be eligible.)
Golf courses, race tracks, and gambling facilities
Churches and church-controlled or fraternal organizations
Lending, investment, and insurance companies|
Projects involving more than $1 million and the relocation of 50 or more jobs

Production agriculture: Eligible only if the farm is vertically-integrated, ineligible for FSA farm loan guarantees, & the agricultural production part of the loan is secondary (less than 50% and less than $1 million). Nursery, forestry, & aquaculture operations are elig ble without these restrictions.

Underwriting and Security Requirements:
- The proposed operation must have realistic repayment ability. - New enterprises may be asked to obtain a feas bility study by a recognized independent consultant.
- The business and its owners must have a good credit history.
- The business must have tangible balance sheet equity position at loan closing/project completion of: 10% or more (for existing businesses) and 20% or more (for new businesses).
- There must be adequate collateral at discounted values.
- Hazard insurance on collateral (lesser of loan amount or depreciated replacement value)
- Key person life insurance may be required (decreasing term OK) – amount negotiated
- Personal/corporate guaranties – normally from all proprietors, partners (except limited partners), or major shareholders (i.e., all those with a 20%-or-greater interest)
- Inability to get credit elsewhere is NOT a requirement.

Application Process: Lender & business submit a joint preapplication to USDA, indicating a willingness to make the loan provided a B&I guarantee is approved. Loans up to $5 million are approved locally; larger ones are approved in Washington, D.C.

USDA B&I Loan Specialists:
Sharon.Exley@wa.usda.gov
Serves Clallum, Island, Kitsap, Jefferson, King, San Juan, Skagit, Snohomish, and Whatcom counties.

Carlotta.Donisi@wa.usda.gov
Serves Clark, Cowlitz, Grays Harbor, Lewis, Mason, Pacific, Pierce, Thurston, and Wahkiakum counties.

Veronica.Baer@wa.usda.gov
Serves Adams, Asotin, Benton, Columbia, Franklin, Garfield, Kittitas, Klickitat, Skamania, Walla Walla, Whitman, and Yakima counties.

Ted.Anderson@wa.usda.gov
Serves Chelan, Douglas, Ferry, Grant, Lincoln, Okanogan, Pend Oreille, Spokane, and Stevens counties.

Margaret.Hair@id.usda.gov
Serves northern Idaho.

Programs:
USDA Cooperative State, Research, Education and Extension
http://www.csrees.usda.gov/
Click on "Quick Links" to Local Extension Office to tap into the huge network of resources for farming, ranching or country living.

State Resources:
Washington State Department of Agriculture
http://agr.wa.gov
360-902-1800

Washington State Agricultural Statistics Service
www.nass.usda.gov/wa
360-902-1940

Idaho State Department of Agriculture
www.agri.state.id.us
208-332-8500

Associations:
Ag Bureau, Greater Spokane Incorporated
www.greaterspokane.org/ag-expo.html
For programs supporting agribusiness
509-321-3633; moleary@greaterspokane.org

Disaster Preparedness

According to Washington State Emergency Management:
Almost 40% of small businesses that close due to a disaster event never re-open. 91% of Americans live in places at moderate to high risk of earthquakes, volcanoes, tornadoes, wildfires, hurricanes, flooding, high-wind damage or terrorism.

Though each situation is unique, any business can be better prepared if it plans carefully, puts emergency procedures in place, and practices for emergencies of all kinds.

Structural Fires
- Install and maintain smoke alarms or a fire suppression system.
- Conduct fire drills regularly.
- Reduce clutter – it is a fuel source and can block exits.
- Take proper precautions regarding smoking and lit candles.

Flooding
- Most standard insurance policies do not cover flood damage and the resulting loss of income. Check with your insurance agent.
- Build with flood-resistant materials to reduce damage.
- Find out the 100-year flood level of your structure.
- Consider working with a licensed contractor to raise electrical and HVAC system above the 100-year flood level mark.
- Raise computers, electronics, and important files off the floor.
- Work with a licensed plumber to install a backflow valve to prevent sewage backup.
- Move critical items above flood level during a flood watch.

Wildfires
- Maintain a 30 foot "combustible-free" zone around your facility.
- Keep grass mowed and irrigated, remove combustible material.
- Build and renovate with flame-resistant materials.
- Keep the roof and gutters clear of debris.
- Attach non-flammable, fine-gauge screening over all chimneys.

Earthquake
- Ensure that your facility is up to code.
- Use natural gas lines with flexible connections and automatic shut-off valves.
- Use flexible water lines and/or couplings to toilets, sinks, and in sprinkler systems.
- Secure equipment to the floor or walls to prevent tipping.
- Make sure anything with a drawer or door, like filing cabinets, has latches with a manual release.

Tornado
- Assign one person to monitor weather alerts.
- Establish interior, preferably basement, locations for employees to gather. Bathrooms, corners, and short hallways are safest.
- Remember, a "watch" means a tornado could happen and a "warning" means you should take immediate cover.
- Keep surplus blankets in a shelter area.

Employees
- Identify an internal shelter incase authorities tell you to "shelter in place".
- Establish a spokesperson to speak to the media and the public.
- Document each employee's job and emergency contact info.
- Decide who is in charge when regular managers are unavailable.
- Create a phone tree and designate individuals who will initiate the communication process.
- Train your employees on the plan and review it with them regularly.

Customers
- Identify the odds that customers will be present if a disaster strikes.
- Keep communications open.
- Keep a copy of your customer records off-site.
- Have an alternate worksite from which to communicate to customers during recovery.

Suppliers
- Maintain a contact list of all your regular suppliers and a backup list of alternates to avoid supply disruption.

Equipment
- Maintain an inventory of all equipment used by your business.
- Keep a maintenance schedule for all equipment, as well as manufacturer and service contact information for each.

Property
- Make sure your facility meets all local building and fire codes.
- Know where utility shutoffs are located and how to operate them.

Records
- Document all processes that make your business run from phones, to finances, to distributing your product or service.
- Develop a schedule for backing up all computer records.
- Keep current copies of paper and computer files off-site.

Insurance
- Insurance coverage can mean the difference between reopening after a disaster strikes or having to close your doors.
- Meet regularly with your insurance agent to ensure you have adequate coverage and knowledge of how to quickly file a claim.
- Consider a policy that will reimburse you for business disruptions in addition to physical losses.

Additional tips
- Get a weather alert radio and monitor it.
- Post emergency numbers and procedures throughout your facility.
- Post evacuation routes and procedures for staff and customers.
- Plan ahead to accommodate individuals with special needs.

Make a supply kit
A well-designed supply kit invaluable during and after a disaster.

- Water	- Duct Tape
- Food	- Radio and batteries
- Tarps	- Cleaning supplies
- First-aid kit	- Flashlights (never use candles or matches)
- Plastic bags	- Gloves (rubber and leather)
- Tool kit	- Camera (to document damage)
- Blankets	

**Advise your employees to store a small supply at work of critical personal items, such as prescription medications.

Important websites

American Red Cross
www.redcross.org

Disaster Assistance
DisasterAssistance.gov

Federal Emergency Management Agency
www.fema.gov/business/guide/index.shtm

Department of Homeland Security
www.ready.gov/business/index.html

Institute for Business and Home Safety
www.disastersafety.org

National Federation of Independent Business
http://www.nfib.com/

UW Emergency Management
http://www.washington.edu/emergency/bcm

Washington State
www.emd.wa.gov/preparedness/prep_business.shtml

Idaho State Bureau of Homeland Security
www.bhs.idaho.gov

Employee vs. Independent Contractor – Ten Tips for Business Owners

If you are a small business owner, whether you hire people as independent contractors or as employees will impact how much taxes you pay and the amount of taxes you withhold from their paychecks. Additionally, it will affect how much additional cost your business must bear, what documents and information they must provide to you, and what tax documents you must give to them.

Here are the top ten things every business owner should know about hiring people as independent contractors versus hiring them as employees.

1. Three characteristics are used by the IRS to determine the relationship between businesses and workers: Behavioral Control, Financial Control, and the Type of Relationship.
2. Behavioral Control covers facts that show whether the business has a right to direct or control how the work is done through instructions, training or other means.
3. Financial Control covers facts that show whether the business has a right to direct or control the financial and business aspects of the worker's job.
4. The Type of Relationship factor relates to how the workers and the business owner perceive their relationship.
5. If you have the right to control or direct not only what is to be done, but also how it is to be done, then your workers are most likely employees.
6. If you can direct or control only the result of the work done -- and not the means and methods of accomplishing the result -- then your workers are probably independent contractors.
7. Employers who misclassify workers as independent contractors can end up with substantial tax bills. Additionally, they can face penalties for failing to pay employment taxes and for failing to file required tax forms.
8. Workers can avoid higher tax bills and lost benefits if they know their proper status.
9. Both employers and workers can ask the IRS to make a determination on whether a specific individual is an independent contractor or an employee by filing a Form SS-8 – Determination of Worker Status for Purposes of Federal Employment Taxes and Income Tax Withholding – with the IRS.
10. You can learn more about the critical determination of a worker's status as an Independent Contractor or Employee at IRS.gov by selecting the Small Business link. Additional resources include IRS Publication 15-A, Employer's Supplemental Tax Guide, Publication 1779, Independent Contractor or Employee, and Publication 1976, Do You Qualify for Relief under Section 530? These publications and Form SS-8 are available on the IRS Web site at **www.irs.gov** or by calling the IRS at 800-829-3676 (800-TAX-FORM).

Business Incubators and Kitchen Centers

AHANA Business Incubator
www.ahana.org
25 W Main, Suite, Spokane WA 99201
509-209-2634

Applied Process Engineering Lab
www.apel.org
350 Hills Street, Suite 101, Richland WA 99354
509-372-5146

Bonner Business Center
www.bonnerbusinesscenter.com
804 Airport Way, Sandpoint ID 83864
208-263-4073

Commercial Kitchen Rental
www.kitchenrental.org
120 E Wellesley, Spokane WA 99207
509-868-5774

Ellensburg BDA Business Incubator
www.kittitascountychamber.com
1000 Prospect, Ellensburg WA 98926
509-925-2002

PAC Business Incubator
www.pacni.org/incubator.html
1100 Airport Drive, Hayden Lake ID 83835
208-772-0584

RCDR Small Business Incubator
www.rcdr.biz
24 South 3rd Ave, Yakima WA 98902
509-453-5133

Sirti Technology Business Incubator
www.sirti.org
665 N Riverpoint Blvd, Spokane WA 99202
509-358-2049

SouthSound Regional Business Incubator
www.ssrbi.com
402 S. 333rd St., Federal Way, WA 98003
253-929-1500

Spokane Entrepreneurial Center
www.spokanecenter.biz
308 W First Ave & 608 W Second Ave, Spokane WA 99201
509-944-0527

Thurston County Small Business Incubator
www.ThurstonIncubator.com
809 Legion Way SE, 3rd Floor, Olympia, WA 98507
360-357-3362

Valley Chamber Business Center
www.spokanevalleychamber.org
1421 N Meadowwood Lane, Liberty Lake WA 99019
9507 East Sprague Avenue, Spokane Valley WA 99206
509-210-2425

Washington CASH Business Accelerator
www.washingtoncash.org
210 24th Avenue S, Suite 380, Seattle WA 98144
206-352-1945

Wenatchee Incubator - Port of Chelan County
125 Easy Street, Wentachee, WA 98801
509-663-5159

William Factory Business Incubator
www.williamfactory.com
1423 East 29th St, Tacoma WA 98404
253-722-5800

Frequently Requested Contacts

Ameritrust	206-402-3971	www.ameritrustcdc.com
Attorney General	800-551-4636	www.atg.wa.gov/
Better Business Bureau	206-431-2222	www.thebbb.org
Business Assistance Hot Line	800-237-1233	
Community Capital Development	206-324-4330	www.seatleccd.com
Dept. of Licensing WA	360-664-1400	www.dol.wa.gov
Dept. of Labor & Industries	360-902-4817	www.lni.wa.gov
Dept. of Labor & Industries	509-324-2600	www.lni.wa.gov
Dept. of Revenue	800-647-7706	http://dor.wa.gov
Equifax	800-685-1111	www.equifax.com
Everett Chamber of Commerce	425-257-3222	www.everettchamber.com
Everett Economic Dev Council	425-743-4567	www.snoedc.org
Everett Dept. of Licensing	425-257-8610	www.ci.everett.wa.us
Evergreen Business Capital	206-622-3731	www.evergreen504.com
Experian	888-397-3742	www.experian.com
FEMA	800-462-9029	www.fema.gov
Insurance Commissioner	360-725-7000	www.insurance.wa.gov
IRS	800-829-1040	www.irs.gov
King County	206-296-1570	www.kingcounty.gov
King County Bar Association	206-623-2551	www.kcba.org
NWBDA	509-458-8555	www.nwbusiness.org
OMWBE	360-753-9693	www.omwbe.wa.gov
Pierce County	253-798-7440	http://co.pierce.wa.us/pc
Procurement Technical Asst Center	425-743-4567	www.washingtonptac.org
SBA Alasksa	800-755-7034	www.sba.gov/ak
SBA Boise	208-334-1696	www.sba.gov/id
SBA Disaster Assistance	800-659-2955	www.sba.gov/disaster
SBA Portland	503-326-2682	www.sba.gov/or
SBA Seattle	206-553-7310	www.sba.gov/wa
SBA Spokane	509-353-2800	www.sba.gov/wa
SBDC Spokane	509-358-7765	www.wsbdc.org
SCORE Bellingham	360-685-4259	bellingham.score.org
SCORE Seattle	206-553-7320	seattle.score.org
SCORE Spokane	509-353-2821	spokane.score.org
SCORE Tacoma	253-680-7770	tacoma.score.org
SCORE TriCities	509-736-0510	midcolumbiatricities.score.org
SCORE Vancouver	360-699-1079	ftvancouver.score.org
SCORE Wenatchee	509-662-2116	centralwashington.score.org
SCORE Yakima	509-248-2021	yakimavalley.score.org
Seattle Chamber of Commerce	206-389-7200	www.seattlechamber.com
Secretary of State WA	360-753-7115	www.sos.wa.gov
Seattle Dept of Licensing	206-684-8484	www.pan.ci.seattle.wa.us
Seattle Library	206-386-4636	www.spl.org
Snohomish County	425-388-3483	www.co.snohomish.wa.us
Spokane Chamber of Commerce	509-624-1393	www.greaterspokane.org
Spokane Dept of Licensing	509-625-6070	www.spokanecity.org
Spokane Library	509-444-5336	http://spokanelibrary.org
Spokane SNAP	509-456-7174	www.snapwa.org
Social Security Administration	800-772-1213	www.ssa.gov
Tacoma Business Center	206-680-7770	
Tacoma Dept of Licensing	253-591-5252	www.cityoftacoma.org
Tacoma Chamber of Commerce	253-627-2175	www.tacomachamber.org
TransUnion	800-888-4213	www.transunion.com
US Customs Service	206-553-0954	www.cbp.gov
US Export Assistance Center	206-553-0051	www.trade.gov
US Pantent & Trademarks	800-786-9199	www.uspto.gov
US Postal Service	800-275-8777	www.usps.com
Washington CASH	206-352-1945	www.washingtoncash.org
WA State Bar Association	800-945-9722	www.wsba.org
WBC Mukilteo	425-423-9090	www.nwwbc.org
WBC Seattle	206-324-4330	www.nwwbc.org
WBC Tacoma	253-680-7770	www.nwwbc.org

Online Information

www.sba.gov/ombudsman
Substantiates and reports to Congress complaints and comments from small business owners regarding unfair regulatory enforcement and compliance activities by federal agencies.

www.sba.gov/ADVO
Serves as the voice of the nation's small businesses, working to reduce the burden that federal policies impose on them, and is the source for small business statistics.

www.epa.gov/smallbusiness/geninfo.htm
General small business and environmental information

www.go2worksource.com
Worksource for Washington employment

www.salaryexpert.com/washington/salary-survey.htm

lmi.idaho.gov/wages/wagesbyoccupation/tabid/749/default.aspx

www.workforceexplorer.com
State Salary and labor market information

www.franchiseregistry.com
The registry lists names of franchise companies whose franchises can be considered for the SBA loan program.

www.ftc.gov
Federal Trade Commission

www.dol.gov/elaws
Helps employers determine which laws administered by the U.S. Dept of Labor apply to their business. Provides compliance information.

www.eeoc.gov
Offers confidential mediation leading to voluntary, negotiated agreements to resolve employment discrimination disputes.

www.foodsafety.gov
The gateway to government food safety Information.

http://www.fmi.org/
The Food Marketing Institute has publications, food and health safety, grocery, demographic and marketing information.

Index

To provide corrections, additions or future updates to this SBA Small Business Resource Guide, contact:
Western Washington: sherry.mina@sba.gov
Eastern Washington and North Idaho: patricia.jordan@sba.gov

Special thanks to Shirley Mylott for content improvements.